HELP! I TEACH CHILDREN'S SUNDAY SCHOOL

3/2001

Help!
I Teach Children's Sunday School

b. max price

SMYTH&HELWYS
PUBLISHING, INCORPORATED   MACON, GEORGIA

faithSteps

Smyth & Helwys Publishing, Inc.
6316 Peake Road
Macon, Georgia 31210-3960
1-800-747-3016

The paper used in this publication meets the minimum requirements of
American National Standard for Information Sciences—
Permanence of Paper for Printed Library Materials.
ANSI Z39.48–1984. (alk. paper)

Library of Congress Cataloging-in-Publication Data

Price, B. Max, 1937–
Help! I teach children's Sunday School / Max Price
p. cm.
ISBN 1-57312-411.7
1. Christian education of children
2. Sunday school teachers
3. Christian education—Activity programs
I. Title.
BV1534.P74 2003
268'.432—dc21

2003002670

Contents

To Geri—lover of children, especially her grandchildren, and my lifelong partner whom I admire and love.

Acknowledgments

For individual contributions of sharing their experiences, wisdom, and expertise in teaching children, I give my appreciation to Darlene Koch, Jennifer Strubhar, Deborah Friant, and Bonnie Blauser. They enriched this book.

Foreword

Teachers in Sunday school and other religious education programs are valuable assets in children's spiritual formations. I salute you. Much of what you do is lay foundations for a child's spiritual growth. This is especially true for infants, toddlers, and preschool children. You are a resource to the child and to the parents and caregivers. Your work is helping children take steps of faith—small and large. You are involved in helping children grow as Jesus did: "Jesus became wise, and he grew strong. God was pleased with him and so were the people." (Luke 2:52). Teaching children is a high calling; teaching children *well* is a great accomplishment. Religious education is the priority of this book. It focuses on the spiritual lives of children—their relationship to God and their relationship with others and self.

Our children live in a changing world. Our challenge is to teach the eternal truth of the gospel with methods that meet the developmental and spiritual needs of today's children.

I am a child psychologist who has been counseling children and their families for more than thirty years. I grew up in small Baptist churches throughout my childhood and adolescence. I served part-time on church staffs for twelve years in positions of associate pastor, youth minister, and mission pastor. I am presently a lay minister in my church in Oklahoma City.

My strong interest in children's spiritual formations led to this book. I offer it as an attempt to help you bless children in your teaching ministry.

Here's to children!

B. Max Price

Parable of the Soils Revisited

Once there was a group of teachers who went out to plant God's message of love and redemption among children. They were full of joy and anticipation as they envisioned eager, young faces waiting to be taught.

They soon became discouraged, however, for it seemed that their words of wisdom fell on minds of short attention span that flew off in all directions. The younger children lived in such a world of make-believe that they thought of Jesus as another Superhero and of heaven as a Disneyland in the sky. The older children's thinking was so concrete that they could not grasp deep, spiritual truths. They would proudly quote the verse "Be ye kind one to another," then turn and punch their neighbor with no evidence of remorse or guilt.

Oh, there were days when the children were attentive and responsive; days in which the word seemed to sprout and grow; days when the children were cooperative. But one hour a week seemed to make so little difference in their lives. School, TV, activities, and family problems choked the message so recently sprouted.

Despite their discouragement, the teachers took another look at their work. They discovered that their task was to prepare the soil, sow the seed, and nurture children so they could grow and develop into spiritual maturity. They sought to understand children—how they think, learn, grow, and develop. They taught children at the level children could understand. They taught the eternal truths with show, tell, and do methods. They bridged church and home by including parents in the religious education program.

So the seed sprouted and grew. And many years later, the seed bore fruit—"some thirty fold, some sixty fold, some one hundred fold."

Chapter One

Today's Children

Teach Your Children Well

There is a great need for effective religious education in the home and in the church. In his book *The School Years*, Dr. Benjamin Spock expressed concern that the American family is being eroded. He stated, "The demands of the workplace and of schools, the excessive mobility of our society, the materialism of our beliefs, the weakening of religious beliefs—these are just few of the changes tugging at the bonds that connect generations." Spock called for emphasis on spiritual values, especially generosity, kindliness, and cooperation. He also stated the importance of religious beliefs and churches' religious education of children.[1]

Our challenge is to teach spiritual values to all children—the good and caring ones and the difficult and hurting ones. People today hunger for spiritual values. They are searching, many in nonreligious areas, to meet their spiritual needs. I believe that the eternal truths of the Bible are valid for today's adults and children. Let us use effective methods to teach these truths to our children and to their parents/caregivers.

If you are reading these words, you likely have a great love for children. You also likely are a talented and dedicated teacher of children in a Sunday school setting. Your task as a teacher is a great one. I commend you for caring and volunteering your time and energy to teach today's children. But who are these children?

Who are Today's Children?

Today's children live in a world of change—the changing family, social and economic change, technological change, and changing environments due to relocation. American children live in varied and complex arrangements. The family has become a more varied institution than it once was. More children are living with only one parent. Even children living with two parents are more likely than before to have stepparents and half brothers/sisters. More children are being raised by their grandparents. Only 59 percent of today's children live in the "traditional family" of twenty-five years ago: two biological parents and only full biological siblings.[2]

Between the 1960s and 1980 the divorce rate doubled, reaching a level where at least one out of two marriages was likely to end in divorce. The divorce rate remained relatively unchanged in the 1980s with a small drop in the 1990s. In addition, an estimated two-thirds of divorcees will remarry. As a result, it has been estimated that 33 percent of all U.S. children will likely live in a stepfamily before age eighteen. It has also been estimated that almost half of children today will spend time in a one-parent family.[3] In 2000, the percentage of all children living in a single-parent family was 27.8.

If you were to teach a Sunday school class of twenty children who were representative of the American family, this is likely what you would find:

• Twelve children would be living with their biological mothers and fathers.
• Five children would be living with a single parent.
• At least two children would be living in a stepfamily.
• At least one child would be living with grandparents.
• Some years you would have adoptive children and foster children in your class.

Are you prepared to teach all of today's children, regardless of their family situations?

Today's Children and Stress

Many children in today's society are overstressed. At any given time, approximately 15 percent of American children need professional counseling for serious behavioral or emotional problems and/or family stress.[4] The causes are multiple:

• Physical and sexual abuse, along with child neglect, traumatize many children. In my home state of Oklahoma, approximately every thirty-four minutes a child becomes a victim of confirmed abuse or neglect. This child abuse rate is close to double what it was in the mid-1980s.

• One in six of America's children live in poverty, according to the 2001 Annie E. Casey Foundation report.[5]

• With the increase in global terrorism and violence in our society, there is a significant increase in children's fears and insecurity.

Are you ready and willing to teach these overstressed and overburdened children?

Practical Exercise

1. List names of children who live in each of the following types of families.

a. Biological parents

b. Stepfamily

c. Single parent

d. Grandparents or other relatives

2. List names of children who have special needs.
   a. New to the community

   b. Health problems

   c. Learning problems

   d. Behavioral or emotional problems

   e. Recent death or loss in the family

   f. Financial needs

   g. Others

3. What are the particular needs of your children?

4. How comfortable are you in teaching this group of children in your Sunday school class?

5. List resources you have in and out of your church to help you with the particular concerns you may face in teaching this group of children.

Notes

[1] Benjamin Spock, M.D., *The School Years* (New York: Pocket Books, 2001), 39-41, 60, 128.

[2] U.S. Bureau of the Census, Current Population Reports, *Marriage, Divorce, and Remarriage in the 1990s* (Washington, D.C.: U.S. Government Printing Office, 1992), 23-180.

[3] *Family and Relationships: Interventions that Work for Stepfamilies* (Washington D.C.: American Psychological Association, 1996).

[4] Max Price, *For Your Child's Sake* (Oklahoma City: self published, 1987), 2-3.

[5] *Kids Count Data Book* (Baltimore: Annie E. Casey Foundation, 2001), 28.

Chapter Two

Characteristics of Effective Sunday School Teachers

Good teachers come in all shapes and sizes, ages and personalities, but certain characteristics separate effective teachers from less effective ones. This section presents skills for which we may strive and in which we may improve.

Effective Teachers Have the Same Spiritual Goal

I suggest our spiritual goals be based on Jesus' statements of the greatest commandments: "'Love the Lord your God with all your heart, soul, and mind.' This is the first and most important commandment. The second most important commandment is like this one. And it is, 'Love others as much as you love yourself'" (Matt 22:37-39).

Goal One: Help children love God.
Goal Two: Help children love others and self.

Our approach to teaching children's Sunday school will be based on the ages and needs of our children, but the overall goals will be the same for infants, toddlers, preschoolers, and school-aged children.

Effective Teachers Know Their Material—the Bible

You do not have to be a Bible scholar to teach children, but it is important that you study and know the biblical material you use in your lessons. Even if the story is familiar, make sure it is interesting and important to you. Study and prepare in order to demonstrate the importantance of this material is to you. When you prepare, you are able to share effectively the moral—the primary lesson the Scripture teaches us.

It is also important for children to memorize Scripture passages and stories. Most of the Bible that I know from memory I learned as a child prior to age twelve.

Effective Teachers Are Good Role Models

I like this quote from Josh Billings: "Train up a child in the way he should go—and walk there yourself once in a while."

A most powerful form of learning at both conscious and unconscious levels is imitation: learning by copying the behavior of significant role models. Children learn much from imitating adults and older children. Recall how many of your own mannerisms and habits were learned from observing your parents. For example, I am always completely dressed before I put on my socks and shoes. That is because I saw my Dad dress this way. I was an adult before I realized the reason I did this. I learned many of my other habits and mannerisms from watching what my parents and other significant adults did.

When you want your children to talk quieter, model soft talking. When you want your children to share, model it. When you want your children to sing joyfully, model it. When you want your children to learn to pray, model it. Children love to act like adults and older children they admire.

Effective Teachers Form Attachments to Their Children

Bonnie Blauser, a gifted Child Development Specialist, shared this wisdom with me: "A child believes, 'What you say about me is what I am. If you treat me with respect, I know that I deserve respect and I develop self-respect. If you accept me for who I really am, I develop self-acceptance. When you value me and recognize my gifts and abilities, I know that I am lovable and capable.' "

Effective teachers genuinely care for children and communicate that caring to them. It is easy to become attached to some of your children. They reach out to you, respond to you, and soak up your caring efforts. Other children are more reserved, aloof, cautious; they are hesitant to trust you or form any kind of closeness. The angry, defiant, resistive children can be difficult because they tend to turn you away with their behavior. They are used to getting negative attention and become quite skilled in dominating the classroom and frustrating teachers. You do not have to like these children, but you are called to love them. This means caring for their welfare, seeking to understand them, and trying to meet their needs whether for more limits, more structure, or more nurturing.

Great teachers form attachments by listening often. They look at their children and listen to them. They "touch base" with their children and try to give each child personal attention each session. I suggest you give each child fifteen to thirty seconds of your complete listening attention each day. That brief amount of time is powerful in the life of a child.

Great teachers visit the children in places other than the classroom. They spend time with them. If you are able to spend special time with each child at least once a year, the child and parents will remember you as a special teacher.

When I was nine years old my Sunday school teacher was Pat Pyron. I remember Pat so many years later because of the way he treated me. I knew I was special to him. He and my parents were friends. He and his wife invited me to their house on numerous occasions. They always had ice cream for me in their freezer. Pat bragged on me and I loved it. He also demonstrated caring and concern for all the children in his class. In Sunday school class, Pat was not a skilled Bible teacher regarding his teaching methods; he was a good teacher because he loved God and showed love and interest in each of us. He was my teacher the year I made my profession of faith. To me, Pat was a special teacher. He is an example of a teacher who formed an attachment to his children.

I knew one first-grade teacher, Mrs. Jackson, who visited in the home of each child at the beginning of the year. In the classroom she had a bulletin board with each child's picture and a paragraph stating something special about that child, such as the name of a pet dog or an activity that the child really liked.

Other good ways to form attachments include calling children on the telephone, mailing them birthday cards, and sending them special notes. Teachers can make a point to notice children and their parents in the church hallways and other meeting areas. For instance, each Sunday I exchange high fives as I meet the children in my church.

Great teaching is love in action. It involves becoming attached to your children and showing it in concrete acts of caring. The children's minister at our church, Jennifer Strubhar, recalled two of her favorite teachers. Her first-grade teacher, Sharon Burns, "made me feel like I was her favorite student. She wrote on all of my school papers, 'I love this paper and the kid who wrote it.' It wasn't until I was older and shared my thoughts with her other students that I realized she made every child feel this way. We each knew we were her favorite."

Virginia Crest was Jennifer's Sunday school teacher in third grade. "She was an excellent listener," Jennifer said. "It felt like she was listening to what each of us had to say about the Bible story. It was like having a talk with your grandmother. She started each week's lesson with songs on her autoharp. She would let us play the autoharp as we sang."

Jennifer said that she couldn't remember any discipline techniques used by either of these two great teachers. "Very little discipline was used; it wasn't necessary because we were so engaged in their classes."

Effective Teachers Create an Environment for Learning

The classroom setting is child-friendly and inviting. When children walk into the room, they recognize it as a place created for them. The room arrangement says, "Come on in! Explore, play, enjoy. I'm glad you're here."

The teacher's body language, words, and actions convey to the children, "I'm here for you. This is your room. This is your time."

A friend of mine, Shrlyn, recalled a favorite teacher who made her classroom special. "In her class, we laughed a lot; we enjoyed being there; we were comfortable in her class. We developed a sense of togetherness from sharing in laughter and learning. It was our class; we belonged together. Our teacher created this wonderful atmosphere. We did not become disruptive or cause behavior problems. We were having so much fun." Shrlyn's eyes sparkled as she recalled this teacher of thirty years ago.

Effective Teachers Understand Their Children's Developmental Levels

There are predictable stages of development for each age in physical, motor, language, cognitive, moral, social, and emotional development. If I understand where a child is in each area of development, I will be better prepared to help him or her make progress to the next level. Children cannot learn until they are developmentally ready. Your children will learn best if you provide a setting that encourages them to grow at their own level.

I have found the Gesell Institute of Child Development to be a great resource in describing characteristics of each age of childhood.[1] Gesell states that there are predictable rhythms of childhood and that the child progresses from alternating stages of equilibrium and disequilibrium. *Equilibrium* refers to a state of balance and relative calm in which the child handles life reasonably well. *Disequilibrium* refers to an alternate stage of imbalance with new growth challenges for mind, body, emotions, and social relations. This rapid stage of change may be quite challenging for the child and for his or her caregivers since the child may be easily upset and more difficult to manage. The good news is that children eventually move from the imbalance of disequilibrium to the next stage of equilibrium: balance. Figures 1 and 2 illustrate these ages of development based on Gesell's and his colleagues' observations.[2]

Figure 1. Alternating Ages of Balance and Unbalance

Ages of Disequilibrium *(off-balance, stormy, rapid change)*	*Ages of Equilibrium* *(balance, calmness, order)*
	10 years
9 years	
	8 years
7 years	
	6 $\frac{1}{2}$ to 7 years
5 $\frac{1}{2}$ to 6 years	
	5 years
4 $\frac{1}{2}$ years	
	4 years
3 $\frac{1}{2}$ years	
	3 years
2 $\frac{1}{2}$ years	
	2 years
18 months	

Figure 2. Alternating Social Ages of Inwardized and Outwardized Behavior

Gesell also describes the child's social development as alternating through stages of inwardized behavior and outwardized behavior.

Inwardized Stages (self-absorbed, pulling away, less friendly)	*Outwardized Stages (outgoing, expansive, friendly)*
	10 years
9 years	
	8 years
7 years	
	6 years
5 years	
	4 years
3 $\frac{1}{2}$ years	
	3 years
2 $\frac{1}{2}$ years	
	2 years
18 months	

It is important for teachers to know the common characteristics of the age group they teach, but two cautions are in order. First, each child is an individual; children behave differently. A child goes through the developmental age levels at his or her own rate. That may be early or late. Second, try to teach each child at his or her developmental level. A child may go through an age level with more or less difficulty based on his or her own temperament, health, family situation, and learning opportunities.

Effective Teachers Recognize Children's Different Areas of Cognitive Strength

Children have different types of cognitive strengths. One child may be gifted in verbal ability, while another child excels in math reasoning. One child's strength may be in understanding people, while another child succeeds at physical activities.

Harvard neurologist Howard Gardner states that there are different kinds of intelligence.[3] He has proposed the existence of at least seven separate forms of human intelligence. Gardner says that most children demonstrate their strengths in one kind of intelligence.

1. *Linguistic Intelligence*—sensitivity to spoken and written language, the ability to learn languages, and skill in expressing oneself with words. Children gifted with linguistic intelligence think in words. They may love to write, read, and spell. As adults, they may be lawyers, speakers, writers, or poets.

2. *Logical-Mathematical Intelligence*—the ability to analyze problems logically, perform mathematical operations, and perform scientific investigation. Children gifted with logical-mathematical intelligence think conceptually. Their strengths are abstract and logical thinking. They use a process of reasoning in their minds, can calculate math problems in their heads, and enjoy computers. As adults, they may be mathematicians or scientists.

3. *Spatial Intelligence*—the potential to recognize and manipulate patterns of wide space as well as patterns of confined areas. Children gifted with spatial intelligence easily locate themselves and other people in space. They are good at mazes and jigsaw puzzles, and they read maps and diagrams easily. As adults, they may be pilots, surgeons, sculptors, architects, or chess players.

4. *Musical Intelligence*—skill in the performance, composition, and appreciation of musical patterns. Children gifted with musical intelligence are especially sensitive to music and other sounds. They remember melodies and learn more easily if material is conveyed to them rhythmically or musically. As adults, they may be musicians or songwriters.

5. *Bodily-Kinesthetic Intelligence*—the potential of using one's whole body or parts of the body to solve problems or fashion products. Children gifted with bodily-kinesthetic intelligence process knowledge through bodily sensations. They excel in sports, are in constant motion, and love physical activities. As adults, they may be dancers, actors, and athletes.

6. *Interpersonal Intelligence*—the capacity to understand the intentions, motivations, and desires of other people and to work effectively with others. Children gifted with interpersonal intelligence understand people and are often leaders among their peers. They are organizers and communicators. They have many friends, are very social, and tend to be "street smart." As adults, they may be salespeople, teachers, clinicians, political leaders, or religious leaders.

7. *Intrapersonal Intelligence*—the capacity to understand oneself and to use such information effectively in managing one's own life. Children gifted with intrapersonal intelligence prefer to be alone with their inner thoughts and feelings. They shy away from group activities. They tend to be strong-willed and march to the beat of a different drummer in their dress styles, behavior, and general

attitudes. As adults, they may be independent thinkers, eccentric individuals, trendsetters, or pioneers.

Everyone has some of all seven kinds of intelligence in varying degrees, but in most people one area dominates. Gardner says that if teachers give students the opportunity to use their bodies, imaginations, and different senses, almost all children will find that they are good at something. Even students who are not outstanding in some area will discover that they have relative strengths.[4]

I recommend that teachers try to understand which kind of intelligence is a child's strength and give the child opportunities to use this ability in class. For example, let the organizer type help you with a class project. Give the child in constant motion an activity that helps the class. Give the word-gifted child an opportunity to write and read for the group. Encourage the musically-gifted to help lead and perform music in the class.

Effective Teachers Use Productive Teaching Methods

As detailed above, because children learn in so many different ways, I recommend *show*, *tell*, and *do* teaching methods.

1. *Show* emphasizes the visual sense. Demonstrate what you want your children to learn. Ours is a visual culture and most children tend to be visual learners. Use visual cues, pictures, demonstrations, and modeling to help them learn.

2. *Tell* emphasizes the auditory sense. Tell your children what you want them to know without using long, drawn-out explanations. Children love stories. They will listen to stories much longer than to plain dialogue. Children love Bible stories and stories with morals. Jesus taught mainly through stories (parables). He used a combination of visual and auditory teaching. His parables painted word pictures of familiar scenes such as fields, plowing, sowing, lakes, fishing, weddings, and meals. When you tell stories, you can use pictures to help children visualize; you can also use word pictures to help children see in their mind a particular place or event.

Adults tend to overuse talking. The best talking, in my opinion, is storytelling with animated demonstration by the teachers and/or the group. Children like for you to be lively and animated when you tell or read them a story. Talk in the way your children can understand. Do not talk longer than their attention spans last.

3. *Do* emphasizes kinesthetic and tactile senses. It is activity-oriented; it is learning by doing and touching. Music and skits (drama) are powerful methods of learning for children.

When you combine show, tell and do in your teaching, you are using effective teaching methods.

My friend Nelda spoke fondly of her religious education experiences as a child, remembering most vividly when her teachers combined visual and auditory senses. She recalled being in the second grade. "I can remember Noah's ark. I can now picture the cutout ark on the flannel board. And I can remember the story of Noah as my teacher told it. The picture of the ark brings out the words of the story. I still remember those scenes."

Nelda loves music and sings in her church's choir. She remembers being three or four years of age and sitting in a worship time. She saw and heard the music director leading a new hymn and watched the pianist play. Nelda said to herself, "I like this," and she began to pretend playing the piano on the back of the pew. She learned the hymn "He Lives" using show, tell, and do methods. She saw the director and pianist leading music, heard interesting words and music, and immediately began the doing activity of singing and playing her pretend piano.

Effective teachers use sound learning methods to teach the gospel.

Effective Teachers Call Forth Children's Gifts

Such teachers look for each child's interests and strengths. They recognize a child's talents often before the child does. Preschoolers and elementary school children form an identity around what they are able to make and do. "Watch me, Mama!" "I can do it." "See what I did."

"I can ride my bicycle without training wheels." "I can do a cart-wheel." "Jim and I made a fort."

Some of your children will not be gifted in reading, or math, or sports, or music, or drawing, or having a vivid imagination, but every child has some talent to be developed. When you encourage a child to express that talent, you put love into action.

When my wife Geri was school-aged, she had a special Sunday school teacher. The teacher recognized Geri's interest and talent in music. She arranged for Geri to come to her house after school, gave her piano lessons without charge, and drove Geri several miles home to her farmhouse. Geri can't remember any great Sunday school lessons her teacher led, but she has lifelong memories of a teacher who demonstrated Christ's love by recognizing a young girl's talent and giving her opportunity to develop her musical ability.

The teaching skills I have listed describe a super teacher. They are descriptions of abilities that great teachers possess. They are goals for which we aim; they are attitudes and skills for which we desire.

You may not be as gifted as you would like, but you do have the capacity to love God and to love others. You also have the opportunity to teach these basic biblical truths to your children. We can say, as Peter and John did in Acts to those who asked for help, "Such as we have, we give to you." Your children have spiritual needs. You have the opportunity and responsibility to help meet their needs.

Blessings, energy, and growth to you!

Practical Exercise

1. Recall a special teacher you had as a child.

• Name of teacher:

• What was unique about him/her?

• Which characteristics of effective teachers did he/she demonstrate?

2. What are your teaching strengths?

3. In which areas do you wish to improve this year?

Notes

[1] Louise Bates Ames and Frances L. Ilg, *Your Five-Year-Old: Sunny and Serene* (New York: Dell Publishing, 1979), foreword.

[2] Louise Bates Ames and Carol Chase Haber, *Your Eight-Year-Old: Lively and Outgoing* (New York: Dell Publishing, 1989), 8, 9.

[3] Howard Gardner, *Intelligence Reframed: Multiple Intelligences for the 21st Century* (New York: Basic Books, 1999), 37-46.

[4] Cited in Thomas Armstrong, *Multiple Intelligences in the Classroom* (Alexandria VA: Association for Supervision and Curriculum Development, 1994), 26-35.

Chapter Three

Birth through Two Years

Babies are such a nice way to start people.

—Carl Sandburg

The main task of teaching infants, toddlers, and two-year-olds is laying the foundations for spiritual development. We do this partly by providing young children developmentally-appropriate experiences. These serve as building blocks for attachment and love, morality, intelligence, and social and emotional well-being.

Well-known pediatrician T. Berry Brazelton, M.D., states,

> At each stage certain experiences are necessary. To learn to relate to others with compassion requires caregivers who provide nurturing, empathetic (understanding) interactions. Learning to read social cues requires that caregivers join in interactive play and negotiations. Creative and logical thinking require that caregivers become partners in pretend play, opinion-oriented discussions and debates . . . . Children master the developmental tasks at very different paces. Hurrying the child through any stage can actually slow him down. The cost is great. A shaky foundation is then built, just as hurrying up the foundation of a house may leave it vulnerable to the first hurricane."[1]

Experiencing trust and security is the primary developmental task during the first year of life. Are the child's physical needs being met? Is the child fed when hungry? Are her diapers changed when dirty? Is he kept warm and dry, touched, cuddled, and held often? Infants sense whether the world wants them, whether it will be responsive to them, and whether it will be a safe place. This occurs at a preconscious level. Creating a trustful and secure environment lays the foundation for the child to be able to trust parents and caregivers, making it easier for him or her to develop trust in God.

Toddlers and two-year-olds have a basic need to develop a sense of self—a sense of being a separate person. Erik Erikson calls this the "autonomy stage" in which the child attains a sense of independence rather than shame and doubt. At this age, children assert themselves with sayings such as "Me do it" and "No." Self-control and willpower are prominent. This stage is sometimes called the "terrible twos" because the loving, cooperative child is now motivated to do things for himself and is often more interested in exploring, holding, throwing, and running than in complying with adult requests. Children at this stage need "child-proof" play areas where they are safe and encouraged to have free, unstructured play.

Teaching this age means close involvement with children's parents. Parents entrust teachers with their precious children. They want to know their children are in a clean, safe environment where teachers will love and care for them. Parents want to be greeted by teachers who listen to their input regarding what their child likes and needs today. Parents need feedback at the end of a session regarding what their child did and learned today. Parents who are satisfied and comfortable with the care their children receive are able to profit more from adult study and worship time. I believe that a significant part of teaching very young children is involvement with parents and caregivers.

Goals

Love God
Help young children learn to trust their environment. Teachers and parents are to meet the physical and safety needs of infants, toddlers, and two-year-olds. Comfort needs, including holding, cuddling, and adult attention and interaction, are also important.

Love Others and Self
Help young children learn to love others and self. Teachers and parents
are to lay the foundations for compassion and caring by meeting the
developmental needs of the first two and a half years of life—trust
and autonomy (gaining a sense of independence and becoming an
individual).

Practical Exercise

Write at least two goals for your children this year.

1. Goal One:

    Objective: How I/we want to accomplish this goal.

2. Goal Two:

    Objective: How I/we want to accomplish this goal.

Common Characteristics of Infants, Toddlers, and Two-year-olds

Birth to One Year

According to John Santrock, the average newborn is twenty inches long and weighs seven and a half pounds. Ninety-five percent of newborns are eighteen to twenty-two inches long and weigh between five and a half and ten pounds.[2]

MOTOR DEVELOPMENT

Santrock describes average motor skills by month:

1st month: Lifts head from a prone position.
3 months: Holds chest up and uses arms for support.
3-4 months: Rolls over.
4-5 months: Supports some weight with legs.
6 months: Sits without support.
7-8 months: Crawls and stands without support.
8 months: Pulls up to a standing position.
10-11 months: Walks using furniture for support.
12-13 months: Walks without assistance.

These are average ages only; the actual time at which these developmental milestones normally occur can vary as much as 2-4 months.[3]

Alex and Alice

At one month, Alice preferred to be held upright so she could see. She became fussy when a teacher held her in a cradle position. Her mother showed the teacher how Alice liked to be held. Then Alice was content.

Four-month-old Alex was lying on his back on the bed. His mother and father were thrilled when all of a sudden Alex rolled over to his stomach. He repeated this three times to the cheers of his parents.

Alice began walking at nine months. Her parents were excited and proud of her accomplishment. They realized that this was an early developmental step, but they did not brag and say that their child was a genius because of early walking.

Alex took his first steps at fourteen months. His parents were worried that he hadn't walked earlier. They were relieved when their pediatrician told them that this was within normal range.

LANGUAGE DEVELOPMENT

From seven or eight months on, babies begin to understand the meaning of their first words. The average one-year-old understands between five and ten words and a few simple instructions such as "sit down," "no," and "wave bye-bye." By three years of age, they understand about 70 percent of the language they will use in ordinary conversation for the rest of their lives. The more caregivers talk to a child, the better. [4]

One-year-old Alex liked to wave "bye-bye" to his Sunday school teacher as he left the room with his father. Three months earlier he ignored his teacher's waving good-bye to him.

SOCIAL DEVELOPMENT

Infants (birth-12 months)

Infants need attachment to caring, attentive adults, most often the mother. Teachers can be extensions of parents' care by holding, touching, talking to, and playing with the child. The key is being responsive to the child's calls for comfort and attention.

Usually friendly Alice went through times of "stranger anxiety" at age seven months. Instead of reaching out to her teacher when brought to class, Alice clung to her mother and cried. Both mother and teacher realized this was a developmental phase in which Alice now noticed familiar faces of Mommy and Daddy, and she recognized non-Mommy faces. This lasted for about six weeks. Then Alice was excited and happy to see her teachers and other family friends.

One-year-olds[5]

At one year of age, many children enjoy a period of calmness and satisfaction. Year-old babies love an audience. They enjoy applause for new abilities such as waving bye-bye or playing pat-a-cake. They like to repeat actions that make adults laugh. They like riding in a stroller, standing, moving toy objects such as cars and balls, and hiding behind chairs and playing "Where's the baby?"

At one, Alex was usually calm and easily satisfied in play, eating, and bedtime. At one and a half, he experienced extreme anger and frustration when he had to stop playing with his favorite toy or when he tried to work a simple puzzle.

The ages of fifteen to twenty-one months tend to be rather difficult. You can expect stormy days at home that, for the most part, children resolve around the time of the second birthday. Wishes and needs are strong but the child often does not have the ability to satisfy these needs.

Eighteen months is an adorable age, but it can also be a difficult one for parents/caregivers and the child. The positive side is that children of this age show overwhelming affection for parents or special toys. They may be extremely lovable to others. At times they love to pick up things for parents and to imitate simple household chores such as sweeping.

Eighteen months is a time when the child is becoming an individual—no longer a baby but not yet a preschooler. Right now the child is emerging; this is often a frustrating time for the child.

According to Louise Bates Ames, soon after eighteen months we see what some have called the truly human thing—that is, the child who begins to behave in particularly human ways. Motor behavior takes over. Children of this age seem to think with their feet. Their behavior is characterized by two extremes: total persistence or the extreme opposite, moving rapidly from one thing to another almost without purpose. Ames describes this child as "walking down a one-way street and his direction tends to be the opposite of what the adult has in mind." At this age, children are extremely self-involved. They relate to others when it pleases them. They tend to be impulsive.[6]

At eighteen months, Alice gave her Mommy a big bear hug when she got out of the car. One second later, she impulsively ran away down the driveway toward the street.

Two-year-olds

Two-year-olds are usually calmer, happier, and emotionally more positive than at age one and a half. Ames labels the two-year-old as "Terrible or Tender."[7]

When Alex's Mom or Dad finish reading a favorite book to him, he repeats "again" over and over. He also wants them to repeat hide and seek again and again and again.

For some parents, two is the best age of all. At two, children have emerged from the impulsive, awkward stage of one and a half years old. Two is often comfortable and content. Life feels good to two-year-olds. They are comfortable with themselves. They are affectionate with parents. There is easy give and take between parent and child.

Two-year-olds can be delightful companions. They like to help with errands. They like to see and touch whatever attracts them until they have had their fill. They like routine and repetition. "Again" is an often-repeated demand.

Two-and-a-half-year-olds

Calmness changes to disharmony. At this age, children often become tense, explosive, and rigid when strong emotions take over. They demand sameness. They want the order in which things are done to be the same. They want things to "stay right there." In contrast to their desire for sameness, children of this age also like to explore and investigate. It's okay for *them* to change things; it's not okay for others to change thing.

This is an age of extremes. Children can be happy and friendly one minute and shy the next. They insist on a special food one minute and reject it the next.

Two-and-a-half-year-old Alice got very upset when her grandparents came for dinner and Grandpa sat in "Daddy's chair." When her parents started to tuck her in bed without singing the good-night song, she became upset again. Rejecting another change to her routine, she threw a temper tantrum.

They can be delightful companions for parents and other adults. Their constant "why" questions can be draining, but they can also provide times of fun and good interaction.

Children of this age become easily frustrated. Almost any restriction of activity or interruptions to their play can be frustrating. Some angry behavior and temper tantrums are common at this age.

The good news is the joy and harmony of the three-year-old is coming.

Remember that these age characteristics are common to particular ages, but each child's developmental level is unique to him or her. Each child is an individual and may develop the same, behind, or ahead of typical schedules.

Teaching Suggestions

1. Refer to the general recommendations for teachers of all ages given in the "General Teaching Suggestions" later in Chapter 8.

2. Help children feel loved and cared for by being responsive to each child's calls for comfort, help, or attention. Hold and cuddle children in the manner they like.

3. Create a clean, safe, and inviting room with age-appropriate toys. Promote trust by being dependable, consistent, nurturing, and responsive to your children.

4. Play with your children. Let them explore and discover toys they like.

5. Model patience and genuine caring for each child.

6. Consult with parents regularly regarding their child's health, mood, likes, and dislikes. Greet parents by name. Give parents brief feedback regarding today's lesson and what their child made or did.

7. Burton White and associates identified three key functions in which effective parents excelled in caring for their young children.[8] I believe these can also apply to teachers.

> (1) They are superb designers and organizers of their child's environment. Have your classroom ready and developmentally appropriate for your children.
> (2) They are firm disciplinarians while at the same time showing great affection for their children. Have consistent limits. Consistently show acceptance and affection.
> (3) They serve as personal consultants to their children in brief episodes of thirty seconds or less. Allow children to initiate most interactions between you and them, but be highly responsive to calls for comfort, information, or a shared enthusiasm.

Plan lesson time for such interactions. You can label times such as song time, story time, play time, snack time, and cleanup time. Children will enjoy the routine and repetition while also experiencing that you are available for them when they need you for a few seconds.

Practical Exercise

Describe two of the children in your class.

1. First child: Name _____ Age _____

   • Describe his/her personality.

• In what ways is he/she similar to the characteristics described above?

• In what ways different?

• What activities does he/she enjoy?

• How well do you think you understand this child? (check one)

Very well _____ Well _____ Average _____ Not Well _____

• What do you think are his/her main needs at this age?

2. Second child: Name _____ Age _____

   • Describe his/her personality.

   • In what ways is he/she similar to the characteristics listed above?

• In what ways different?

• What activities does he/she enjoy?

• How well do you think you understand this child? (check one)

Very well _____ Well _____ Average _____ Not Well _____

• What do you think are his/her main needs at this age?

Notes

[1] T. Terry Brazleton, M.D., and Stanley I. Greenspan, M.D., *The Irreducible Needs of Children: What Every Child Must Have to Grow, Learn, and Flourish* (Cambridge MA: Perseus, 2000), 115, 116.

[2] John W. Santrock, *Life-Span Development*, 7th ed. (Boston: McGraw-Hill College, 1999), 22.

[3] Ibid., 131.

[4] Burton L. White, *The New First Three Years of Life* (New York: Simon & Schuster, 1995), 22.

[5] Louise Bates Ames, *Your One-Year-Old: Fun-Loving and Fussy* (New York: Dell, 1982), 11, 16, 17.

[6] Ibid., 11, 13.

[7] Louise Bates Ames, *Your Two-Year-Old: Terrible and Tender* (New York: Dell, 1976), 8-18.

[8] *APA Monitor* (July 1976): 4, 5.

Chapter Four

Three through Five Years

Goals for Spiritual Development

Love God

1. Foster in your children a sense of security that God loves them. "We love him because he first loved us" truly applies to preschool children. They need to experience being loved by adults so they can respond back in love. These children need to hear the stories of grace that God loves them.

2. Help children learn to worship God through prayers, singing, and Bible stories.

3. Help children learn to love God's creation. Nature with all its glory is a tangible expression of God's work. Loving God's world is an important step in learning to love God.

Love Others and Self

1. Teach your children the spiritual values of generosity, cooperation, and kindness. You can model these virtues in the way you treat the children and other adults. Children also learn through practice in their social interaction with other children and adults. Teachers can lay the groundwork with preschool children so that these values may grow stronger as children mature.

2. Provide children the experience of being valued, respected, cared for, and treated as capable by their teachers and parents/caregivers. Preschoolers are active and curious. Teachers and parents/caregivers

can provide them the security of being loved. Allow children to express their strong needs to explore, question, and initiate activities.

Too much criticism and restriction stifles children's creativity and learning. Such actions can teach guilt and lack of self-confidence and give the message that "there's something wrong with you."

Too much freedom ignores preschoolers' need for adult supervision and interaction. Children need limits. They need to know what the rules are and that there are adults who care enough about them to set necessary limits. A child who is frequently criticized by significant adults or who does not have good supervision is not a happy child.

Practical Exercise

Write at least two goals for your children this year.

1. Goal One:

Objective: How I/we want to accomplish this goal.

2. Goal Two:

Objective: How I/we want to accomplish this goal.

Common Characteristics of Children Ages Three to Five

Preschool children are very active. They are curious about the world, and they love to explore it. Play is a vital way that children learn and express themselves. Play is the language of children this age, and toys are their words. Threes to fives ask many why questions. They like to run and do. They like to make things. They tend to interpret life from their limited experience.

Preschoolers are literal in their reasoning. They also practice magical thinking. Children often believe that if they are called a certain name such as "Stupid" or "Smart," they magically take on the characteristics associated with the name. They believe events that happen together cause one another. A child can become attached to a blanket or teddy bear that on one occasion was associated with comfort and good feelings. Thus the blanket "causes" good feelings. Such magical thinking makes children believe they are responsible for a good or bad event. For example, a child may believe that she did or said something that caused her parents to separate. Another child may believe that he did or said something that made a sick family member well.

Preschoolers find it hard to share, and not only because they are selfish. They think of their possessions as being an actual part of themselves.

A major developmental need of this age is to develop a sense of initiative, curiosity, and exploration rather than a strong sense of guilt for bothering adults by asking so many questions or wanting adults to play with them, causing too many problems, or making their parents mad.

PHYSICAL DEVELOPMENT

The average child grows two and a half inches in height and gains five to seven pounds a year during early childhood. Growth patterns vary by individual. Differences in weight are due primarily to genetics, nutrition, and ethnic origin. The brain is a key aspect of growth. By age five, the brain has reached 90 percent of its adult size.

Bo and Bonnie

Three-year-old Bonnie's height and weight are above average. Her parents' height, both above average, and the family's healthy nutrition habits contribute to Bonnie's size.

At age four, Bo's brain has grown to the degree that his eye-hand coordination is significantly improved since he was a two-year-old.

Three-year-old Bonnie can ride a tricycle, build block towers, and complete jigsaw puzzles.

Four-year-old Bo loves to climb on anything, loves to build houses or churches with blocks, and enjoys drawing.

MOTOR DEVELOPMENT

Gross and fine motor skills increase dramatically. These children are the most active of any age group. They are curious about the world and eager to explore it. They run easily, climb a ladder to a slide, and move quickly from one activity to another.

LANGUAGE DEVELOPMENT

At age three, children move from words to sentences. They talk to themselves out loud. They tend to talk constantly. Words become meaningful. They love new words and big words.

COGNITIVE DEVELOPMENT

Cognitive development in this age group is characterized by "magical thinking": a belief that their thoughts or actions can make things happen. Vivid imagination with pretend friends and/or animals is common. They have the mental ability to have an object represent

Three-year-old Bonnie talks to herself while she is playing, eating, and enjoying other activities. At age four she asks "why" questions over and over.

Five-year-old Bo loves for someone to read to him; he is eager to learn to read.

someone or something that is not present, such as a scribbled design being "Mommy." They begin to classify objects such as circles or squares. They develop beginning reasoning powers but do not grasp the concept of object permanence: that objects remain the same even if you change the form.

MORAL/ETHICAL DEVELOPMENT

We see signs of conscience that may be severe at times and lacking at other times. Conscience is a repository of moral values and sense of right and wrong. It is greatly influenced by parents'/caregivers' approval and disapproval of certain behaviors. A good conscience operates like a good and effective parent.

SOCIAL/EMOTIONAL DEVELOPMENT

Ames and Ilg refers to the three-year-old as "Friend or Enemy."[1] Most three- to five-year-olds have a good self-concept, are cooperative, want to please, and like friendly humor. They are responsive to praise and compliments. They enjoy other children and especially enjoy their mother/primary parent. They are usually happy kids. At three and a half, the opposite often happens. Children of this age frequently refuse simple commands and tend to be inwardized, insecure, anxious, and self-willed. They are emotionally inconsistent. Ames and Ilg label the four-year-old as "Wild and Wonderful."[2] For the most part they are joyous, exuberant,

Four-year-old Bonnie was given two identical pieces of clay. After she watched her mother flatten one piece, Bonnie was asked if they were still the same. Bonnie said, "No, this one [the fatter piece] is bigger."

Five-year-old Bo is fascinated with super-heroes. One day he announces he is Superman, another day he is Spider-Man.

Four-year-old Bonnie controls her desire to get food out of the refrigerator in the morning but not later in the day.

Five-year-old Bo knows it is "bad" to play in the street because he could get hurt, but without supervision he is likely to play there anyway.

and ready for anything. They love adventure, excitement, and anything new. They are responsive to adults. Four year-olds' emotions are extreme—they love a lot, dislike a lot. They have vivid imaginations and enjoy children their age. Ames and Ilg calls five-year-olds "Sunny and Serene."[3] Five-year-olds want to be good and often are. They enjoy life, are optimistic, and often ask for permission. They especially want to please parents, grandparents, and other significant adults. At five and a half they are ready to disobey, to be brash and combative.

> At three, Bonnie likes to play with other children in Sunday school. This week she asked a classmate, "Can I play with you?" At three and a half she sometimes regresses to "baby talk" and clutches her security blanket. This morning she argued with her mother over getting dressed for church.
>
> At four, Bo is irrepressible. Tonight his mother's ears are hurting from his many "why" questions and his nonstop talking. At five and a half, Bo has suddenly changed from a wonderful, fun-loving, easily-managed five-year-old to an arguing, openly-defiant child. Today he argued for fifteen minutes about doing his daily chores.

Practical Exercise

Describe two of the children in your class.

1. First child: Name _____ Age _____

   • Describe his/her personality.

   • In what ways is he/she similar to the characteristics listed above?

• In what ways different?

• What activities does he/she enjoy?

• How well do you think you understand this child? (check one)

Very well _____ Well _____ Average _____ Not Well _____

• What do you think are his/her main needs at this age?

2. Second child: Name _____ Age _____

• Describe his/her personality.

• In what ways is he/she similar to the characteristics listed above?

• In what ways different?

• What activities does he/she enjoy?

• How well do you think you understand this child? (check one)

Very well _____ Well _____ Average _____ Not Well _____

• What do you think are his/her main needs at this age?

Teaching Suggestions

1. Refer to the general recommendations for teachers of all ages given in the "General Teaching Suggestions" of chapter 8.

2. Focus on activities for this active age group. Most love singing, simple drama, or role-playing Bible characters and other significant people.

3. Use many visuals and demonstrations. Most children are visual learners and need you to show them what you want them to learn.

4. Teach the children simple worship activities like praying, thanking God, giving, and sharing with others.

5. Talk to the children in literal descriptive language. When you use important abstract words such as truth, justice, lying, grace, freedom, and righteousness, use descriptions and examples. For instance, "God loves you this much (hands spread wide). Even when we do something God told us not to, like hit another child, God still likes us. The word for this is grace."

6. Work with parents/caregivers. Ask them for information about their child—likes, dislikes, how the child feels today. Give parents feedback as often as possible. Tell them what the class did and something their child did today. Describe the child's activities. Try to give them at least two positive things this child did for each negative behavior. Do not let negative behavior build up so that one week you surprise caregivers with a list of problematic actions the child has done on several occasions. For problem behaviors, ask caregivers advice about what has worked and not worked at home.

7. Work on team building with your fellow teachers. Share information, plans, and support with other teachers. Keep learning. If you need to learn more about certain areas, seek resources from other teachers and children's ministers.

8. Value your contribution to shaping the spiritual lives of children.

Notes

[1] Louise Bates Ames and Frances L. Ilg, *Your Three-Year-Old: Friend or Enemy* (New York: Dell, 1976), 1-12.

[2] ———, *Your Four-Year-Old: Wild and Wonderful* (New York: Dell, 1976), 1-13.

[3] ———, *Your Five-Year-Old: Sunny and Serene* (New York: Dell, 1979), 1-11.

Chapter Five

Six through Seven Years (First and Second Graders)

Goals for Spiritual Development

Love God

1. Teach children the biblical view of God at the level they can understand.
   - *As Creator.* God made the world and keeps it going.
   - *As Loving Parent.* God loves us, takes care of us, wants what is best for us, and corrects us when we disobey.
   - *As Redeemer.* God sent Jesus to die for us, to forgive us when we do wrong, and to show us how to live.
   - *As Holy Spirit.* Jesus lives in our hearts.

2. Help children worship God through praying, singing, learning Bible stories, and celebrating with art and drama.

3. Help children learn to love God by loving God's creation. Help develop their sense of wonder and awe at the beauty of God's creation. Nature is a visible expression of God's power and glory. As the psalmist declares, "The heavens keep telling the wonders of God, and the skies declare what he has done. Each day informs the following day; each night announces to the next." (Ps 19:1-2).

Love Others and Self

1. Help children to love and respect themselves and each other. Share the biblical teaching that God loves them no matter what, that each child is special to God, that each child has something he or she can do well, and that we sometimes do wrong but God will forgive us.

2. Provide children the experience of being valued, respected, cared for, and treated as capable by their teachers and parents/caregivers. First and second graders are active, eager to learn, concerned about pleasing significant adults, and learning rules of right and wrong. They need opportunities to show what they can do and to receive our approval and blessing.

3. Teach spiritual values of generosity, cooperation, kindliness, and honesty.

   Generosity. Take advantage of six- and seven-year-olds' impulse to be helpful and giving. They can be led into acting friendly toward people who are different from them. They can learn to be tolerant, a vital part of generosity. Children at this age can be encouraged to think generously outside their own circle. They can be led to give some of their money to church and other charities, to give away toys and clothes they have outgrown, and to volunteer to help others. Our goal is to help children experience the joy of generosity versus the selfishness of greed.

   Cooperation. Give children opportunities to be helpful and to have joint activities that foster cooperation. Children need adults to model cooperation and give them practice in working together. Adults can use their speech and actions to show children that cooperation is expected.

   Kindliness. This spiritual value emphasizes being polite, loving, and caring toward others. It rejects society's emphasis on children being completely self-sufficient without concern for the needs of others. Excessive selfishness and greed are significant values in today's culture. A focus on the spiritual values of kindness and generosity is a major need in children's religious education.

   Honesty. Adults can model honesty in their relationship with children, compliment children when they show courage in telling the truth, share stories that demonstrate honesty, and lead discussions regarding the importance of telling the truth.

Practical Exercise

Write at least two goals for your children this year.

1. Goal One:

   Objective: How I/we want to accomplish this goal.

2. Goal Two:

   Objective: How I/we want to accomplish this goal.

Common Characteristics of Children Ages Six and Seven

Child behavior develops in a particular pattern. Children go through predictable stages of development. The following characteristics are to help you know what to expect in your children at certain ages. However, each child progresses at his or her own rate depending on personality, health, and how the world treats him or her. An individual child may be at a younger or older level of development.

The following are common characteristics of most six- and seven-year-olds. Ames and Ilg describe the six-year-old as "loving and defiant."[1] Early six-year-olds can be a "handful," and six-and-a-half-year-olds can be "truly gorgeous." Seven-year-olds are described as living "life in the minor key."[2] Seven is a sober, thoughtful, self-absorbed age.

Six-year-olds

In general, six is an active, outgoing age in which children are quite
self-centered. They change rapidly, growing more mature, more independent, more daring, and more adventurous. Being six is not
necessarily an easy time for a child. Six-year-olds are highly active, in
constant motion, shoving, pushing, and talking. Sitting or standing,
six-year-olds wiggle and squirm. Boisterous play and verbal aggression
such as "You stink" and "You're stupid" are common. Making things is
a preferred activity. Six-year-olds tend to be assertive, bossy, and
extremely sensitive to real or imagined slights such as another child
getting a larger piece of cake. They tend to be dawdlers, such as being
slow to get dressed for the day or to clean their room. They can be
affectionate and loving. Six-year-olds like to go places and do things
with parents, especially father figures.

Typical six-year-olds seem to live at opposite extremes. They find
it hard to choose. "I want to and I don't want to" is a common feeling
when faced with a decision or adult request. Children of this age are
often stubborn. They want to be first and best; they want to win and
have the most of everything. Enthusiasm is an enduring trait. Six-year-
olds can be demanding and difficult, but when their needs are met,
there are no better, warmer, more enthusiastic companions. They can
be warm, friendly, delightful, and a joy. At six-and-a-half years, all the
lively, exuberant responses characteristic of this age tend to come to
fruition.

Seven-year-olds

Seven tends to be a quiet and subdued age. Seven-year-olds are sober
and thoughtful. They are quieter when contrasted with their lively
behavior at age six. The boisterous activity of age six is replaced with
high mental activity. Seven-year-olds are less selfish than at six but
extremely self-absorbed. They are sensitive to the reactions of others—
what other children, parents, and teachers say and do. They frequently
complain about being treated unfairly. They often worry that someone
doesn't like them.

Seven-year-olds tend to show politeness and consideration toward
adults that was rare at age six. They like to be helpful at home, school,

and church. They wish for perfection. They have high standards for themselves and do not want to make any mistakes. Seven has been called "the eraser age" because the child keeps working until the job is finished, with many erasures, to get the paper just right.

Six-year-olds are attackers. They like to start things. Seven-year-olds are finishers. They want to make a place for themselves at home and school. A primary developmental task of these children is to be industrious. Their identity and sense of self worth tend to be tied to what they can do and make.

PHYSICAL DEVELOPMENT

Children ages six to seven experience slow, consistent growth. They grow an average of two to three inches per year and gain approximately five to seven pounds per year. Exercise is important through play and sport activities. A significant percent of children are physically out of shape and overweight due to lack of exercise and poor diet.

MOTOR DEVELOPMENT

Children's motor development becomes smoother and more coordinated during these years. Physical activity is essential for children to refine their gross and fine motor skills. Elementary children are far from physically mature and they need to be active. They become more fatigued by long periods of sitting than by running, jumping, or bicycling.

Cal and Calista

Six-year-old Calista is constantly active. She enjoys active play, dancing, learning gymnastics, and running everywhere.

Seven-year-old Cal is much better coordinated than he was a year ago. For exercise he rides his bike, climbs trees, and plays basketball with his friends and family.

LANGUAGE DEVELOPMENT

Six-year-olds love to talk. They enjoy learning new words and are proud of any beginning reading abilities. Most have good pronunciation and fairly accurate grammar.

Six-year-old Calista likes to tell her parents how high she can count and that she can read some words in her favorite book.

Seven-year-old Cal likes to use adverbs such as "actually," "remarkably," and "surprisingly."

Seven-year-olds try to say things just right and want others to say things just right. They are interested in the meaning and spelling of words and like to use pictorial dictionaries. They enjoy phone conversations. They have an expanded use of adverbs.

COGNITIVE DEVELOPMENT

Six-year-olds are approaching the age of reason. They are at the end of preoperational thinking in which they are the center of the world. They can reason in their heads in more than simple trial-and-error activity. They can classify objects by shape, size, or color.

Piaget's concrete operational stage begins around age seven. Most seven-year-olds can see the ways that objects are alike and different: apples and oranges are both food; they're both fruit; one is red and the other is orange. They can begin to see how a fish and a submarine are alike and different: they both go under water, but a submarine is a kind of boat and a fish is a water animal.

Six-year-old Cal is presented plastic blocks of different shapes, sizes, and colors. When he is asked to take all the red, round ones, Cal looks and thinks of two classes—color and shape—as he selects only the correct blocks. If he is asked to find all the small, blue, square ones, Cal is likely to have some trouble thinking correctly of three classes— size, shape, and color.

Seven-year-old Calista is presented with the same situation she had at age four. She is given two identical pieces of clay. She watches her mother flatten one piece. When asked whether the two pieces are alike or the same, Calista says the pieces are still the same size even after the shape of one piece changed.

MORAL/ETHICAL DEVELOPMENT

For the six-year-old, goodness is what his parents and teachers approve of or require and badness is what they disapprove of or forbid. Children of this age sometimes take things that aren't theirs, and they don't always tell the truth. Good ethical behavior usually comes later than six.

Seven-year-olds have definite ethical standards and try hard to do good and avoid doing bad. They try to tell the truth and avoid taking things that belong to others. Fairness is important to seven-year-olds. They also believe firmly and without question what they have been taught about God.

Six-year-old Cal's list of good things to do includes keeping quiet and answering people when they talk to him and going to bed at 7:30. Bad things not to do, according to Cal, include asking for the biggest piece of something and pinching people.

Seven-year-old Calista is beginning to generalize the concepts of goodness and badness. For her, selfishness is thinking only of herself, such as speaking rudely to her mother. Unselfishness is thinking about others, such as not shouting in the library.

SOCIAL/EMOTIONAL DEVELOPMENT

According to Erik Erikson, a dominant theme of childhood is industry versus inferiority.[3] Industry refers to the ability to do something well. First and second graders like to make, build, and work. They become interested in how things are made and how things work. Children's competence increases when they are encouraged in their efforts to build things such as models or playhouse, and to work at tasks such as reading, solving problems, and cooking.

When children are criticized for their efforts by parents, teachers, and other significant adults, they tend to develop a sense of inferiority. Elementary school years are a critical time in developing a positive or negative self-concept. Self-concept refers to how a child thinks and feels about herself—whether she sees herself as able to do a job well or thinks whatever she undertakes will end badly; whether she thinks of herself as capable or incapable, good or bad, liked or disliked.

This is a time of partial separation from parents and the beginning of new attachments to other adults and peers. During these years, children often idolize their teachers and famous people. Making friends is an important task at this age. Children begin to form "chumships" (close friendships), usually with a child of the same sex. It is a time of learning rules—rules for how to treat others; rules for obeying teachers; and rules for reading, writing, and arithmetic. Boys are usually more aggressive and active than girls. Girls usually have more self-control than boys. Boys tend to play in large groups, and their games have winners and losers. Girls are more likely to play in small groups with friends and taking turns more prominent than winning or losing.

A child's emotional intelligence is a good predictor of his or her success in life, according to Daniel Goleman.[4] Emotional intelligence refers to a child's ability to recognize emotional impulses, to have self-control, to use the people skills of empathy and graciousness, to read social situations, and to delay gratification.

Calista is having behavior problems: she throws a fit when her team loses at recess. She has trouble keeping friends because of her anger and gets very upset when she has to wait her turn. Calista's family has emphasized how gifted and smart their daughter is, but they have neglected emotional intelligence skills.

Cal's positive self-concept has been displayed this year in his willingness to study hard to improve his reading, in which he is a slightly behind. He has an "I can do it" attitude regarding learning to ride a bike and skate. He is positive about his ability to adjust to his family's move to a new city and new school. His parents are encouragers. Cal's Sunday school teachers quickly include him in doing tasks. Last Sunday he played Moses in the lesson about the Ten Commandments.

Practical Exercise

Describe two of the children in your class.

1. First child: Name _____ Age _____

- Describe his/her personality.

- In what ways is he/she similar to the characteristics listed above?

- In what ways different?

- What activities does he/she enjoy?

- What are his/her strengths (things he/she can do well)? What are his/her difficulties (things he/she has a hard time doing)?

- How well do you think you understand this child? (check one)

Very well _____ Well _____ Average _____ Not Well _____

• What do you think are his/her main needs at this age?

2. Second child: Name _____ Age _____

   • Describe his/her personality.

   • In what ways is he/she similar to the characteristics listed above?

   • In what ways different?

   • What activities does he/she enjoy?

   • What are his/her strengths (things he/she can do well)? What are his/her difficulties (things he/she has a hard time doing)?

   • How well do you think you understand this child? (check one)

Very well _____ Well _____ Average _____ Not Well _____

What do you think are his/her main needs at this age?

Teaching Suggestions

1. Refer to the general recommendations for teachers of all ages given in the "General Teaching Suggestions" of chapter 8.

2. Provide freedom within limits. First and second graders are active and have difficulty with self-control. They are old enough to understand the rules—for home, school, and church. I suggest that you provide the fewest rules possible, but give as many as necessary for your class. Have the rules written and repeat them to children as often as necessary. In my counseling with children, I tell the child at his first appointment, " I have two main rules: (1) When you finish playing with something, put it away before you get something else. (2) No hitting, kicking, or spitting." Most children comply with these rules the first time. Surprised parents have observed their child putting toys away without being told and have said, "He doesn't do this well at home." Once the boundaries (the don'ts) are established, I recommend focusing on the dos of behavior, such as waiting your turn, sharing, controlling your hands, and putting things away.

3. Try to form an attachment to your children. Don't rush them. Show interest in what they do. Look for moments to share and to show caring.

4. Try to meet the children's primary needs: making, doing, building, and working. Design your teaching to include activities for these active children. Give them encouragement and recognition for their efforts. Use drama, skits, music, and art in your instruction. You do not have to be gifted in music, art, and drama to teach your children well. Give them opportunities to express themselves—to make and

do. Demonstrate your interest, caring, and encouragement. Let them know by your words and actions that you like them and like their work. For instance, say, "Dawnn, I really like the way you drew Mary and baby Jesus. You are good at drawing." Or "Tyrone, thank you for asking Ben to sit by you and for being his friend today."

Abraham Lincoln said, "It is difficult to make people miserable when they feel worthy of themselves." This applies to children who feel competent and sense that they are loved by parents, family, teachers, and God.

5. Peer and friendship skills are strong needs of this age. Emphasize the spiritual values of being nice, treating others kindly, and sharing.

6. Provide emotional support by listening to, encouraging, and helping children, especially when they are upset, discouraged, sad, or anxious.

7. Include children's concerns in your group prayer time. Let them share praises of something good that has happened and any worries, sicknesses, or sad times.

8. Teach children the biblical view of people: the good news that they were made in the image of God and that each child is very special to God. We were made with the ability to be creative and the ability to know and love God and others. The bad news is that we all do wrong. We all sin, but God forgives us when we ask. Teach grace with practical examples, words, and activities that children can understand.

9. Make the children's class a haven for them.

10. Provide enough sameness so children can feel comfortable and have a routine. When they feel secure in your classroom, children will have more energy for learning what you want to teach them. Many of our children are overstressed from family problems and overly busy with after-school activities.

11. Share information with parents/caregivers regarding the lessons you will be teaching. Tell them what their child did and made during your teaching session.

Notes

1 Louise Bates Ames and Frances L. Ilg, *Your Six-Year-Old: Loving and Defiant* (New York: Dell, 1979), 1-13.

2 ———, *Your Seven-Year-Old: Life in a Minor Key* (New York: Dell, 1985), 1-17.

3 Cited in John W. Santrock, *Life-Span Development*, 7th ed. (Boston: McGraw-Hill College, 1999), 34-37.

4 Ibid., 326, 327.

Chapter Six

Eight through Nine Years (Third and Fourth Graders)

Goals for Spiritual Development

Love God.

1. Teach children the biblical view of God at the level they can understand.

   • *As Creator.* God made the world and keeps it going.

   • *As Loving Parent.* God loves us, takes care of us, wants what is best for us, and corrects us when we disobey.

   • *As Redeemer.* God sent Jesus to die for us, to forgive our sins, and to show us how to live.

   • *As Holy Spirit.* Jesus lives in our hearts.

2. Help children worship God through praying, singing, learning Bible stories, and celebrating with art and drama.

3. Lead children to a personal experience of trust in Christ. You sow the seed of the gospel at this age so that the children will take faith steps in giving themselves to God.

4. Help children love God by loving God's creation. Help develop their sense of wonder and awe at the beauty of God's creation. The earth and the sky belong to God. They are visible expressions of God's power and glory. As the psalmist declares, "The earth and everything in it belong to the LORD" (Ps 24:1a); "The heavens keep telling the wonders of God, and the skies declare what he has done (Ps 19:1).

Love Others and Self

1. Help children love and respect themselves. Share the biblical teaching that God loves them no matter what, that each child is special to God, that each child has something he or she can do well, that even though we do wrong, God will forgive us.

2. Provide children the experience of being valued, respected, cared for, and treated as capable by their teachers and parents/caregivers.

3. Teach the spiritual values of generosity, cooperation, kindliness, and honesty.

    Generosity. Provide eight- and nine-year-olds experiences in giving. They can be led into acting friendly toward people who are different from them. They can learn to be tolerant, a vital part of generosity. Children at this age can be encouraged to think generously outside their own circles. They can be led to give some of their money to church and other charities, to give away toys and clothes they have outgrown, and to volunteer to help others. Our goal is to help children experience the joy of generosity versus the selfishness of greed.

    Cooperation. Give children opportunities to be helpful and to have joint activities that foster cooperation. Children need adults to model cooperation and give them practice in working together. Adults can use their speech and actions to show children that cooperation is expected.

    Kindliness. This spiritual value emphasizes being polite, loving, and caring toward others. It rejects society's emphasis on children being completely self-sufficient without concern for the needs of others. Excessive selfishness and greed are significant values in today's culture. A focus on the spiritual values of kindness and generosity is a major need in children's religious education.

    Honesty. Adults can model honesty in their relationship with children, compliment children when they show courage in telling the truth, share stories that demonstrate honesty, and lead discussions regarding the importance of telling the truth.

Practical Exercise

Write at least two goals for your children this year.

1. Goal One:

Objective: How I/we want to accomplish this goal.

2. Goal Two:

Objective: How I/we want to accomplish this goal.

Common Characteristics of Children Ages Eight and Nine

Child behavior develops in a particular pattern. Children go through predictable stages of development. The following characteristics are to help you know what to expect in your children at certain ages. However, each child progresses at his or her own rate depending on personality, health, and how the world treats him or her. An individual child may be at a younger or older level of development.

The following are common characteristics of most eight- and nine-year-olds. Ames and Haber describe the eight-year-old as "lively and outgoing."[1] Eight-year-olds are constantly on the go and ready for action. They work fast, play fast, and eat fast. They relate to people more easily than at age seven. Nine-year-olds are described as "thoughtful and mysterious."[2] Their behavior tends to be uneven and unpredictable. Children of this age may act one way one day and the opposite on another day.

Eight-year-olds

Eight-year-olds tend to be much more outgoing than seven-year-olds. They have high energy and seem willing to tackle almost anything, even new and difficult activities. They love to talk. They show interest and enormous curiosity in the world—both the here and now and in historical events and people. They are a collector of things.

Eight-year-olds also tend to be judgmental and critical both of others and self, but they are sensitive about being criticized. They want to know the "why" of events.

Seeing and being with friends is extremely important at this age. There is a noticeable separation between the sexes with an attitude of both attraction and hostility toward the opposite sex. There is often much less playing with children of the opposite sex at age eight.

Nine-year-olds

Much of the behavior of nine-year-olds is uneven and unexpected. These children are more independent and self-motivated. They wish to do things their own way and in their own time. They wish to be free of adult supervision. Ames and Haber state that nine-year-olds are emerging from strong preoccupation with their mother (or caregiving parent). At eight, children cannot get enough of mother; at nine, they often like to be away from her presence and sometimes resent her demands.[3]

Nine-year-olds tend to be less secure than eight- or ten-year-olds. They are often more anxious, more withdrawn, and less certain. Nine-year-olds take themselves and their activities seriously and want to do things right. Their interests are varied and so numerous that their days may be too full.

Nine-year-olds may worry and complain often. They tend to be responsible, enjoy learning, and love to talk with friends. Disgust for the opposite sex is common. Many boys will have nothing to do with girls and girls may refer to boys as "gross." As they move toward age ten, children usually reach the high point of childhood. Ten-year-olds are usually quite secure and self-confident. Life can be relatively calm for the ten-year-old with no major challenges; the stresses of adolescence are not yet present. David Elkind states, "The ten-year-old is at peace with himself and his world."[4]

It is important not to rush the nine- and ten-year-old into adolescent interests and activities, despite the commercial pressure to look and act like a teenager.

PHYSICAL DEVELOPMENT

Children grow an average of two to three inches a year. Muscle mass and strength gradually increase. Legs lengthen. Growth is slow and consistent.

MOTOR DEVELOPMENT

Motor skills become smoother and more coordinated. Children's lives need to be activity-oriented for motor development. Boys are usually better at gross motor skills. Girls are usually better at fine motor skills.

LANGUAGE DEVELOPMENT

Typical eight-year-olds love to talk. They use language fluently. They speak in their ordinary English (or other native language) but are also interested in code language such as Pig Latin or the use of secret passwords. They are capable of good pronunciation and fairly good use of grammar.

Eight-year-olds seem to talk simply for the sake of hearing themselves talk. At age nine, children use language more as a tool to share ideas, state opinions, and express feelings and self-criticism. Nine-year-olds use less wild exaggeration and tall tales. They show more interest in the real world and less interest in fairy stories.

David and Davina

Davina is generally in good health. However, when she is fatigued from too much activity, considers something too difficult to do, or faces stressful family situations, she tends to complain of stomachaches or other body pains.

Eight-year-old Davina is proud of her ability to draw and write. She wrote and drew a picture-story birthday card for her grandfather.

Nine-year-old David can run fast. He can catch and throw a football much better than when he was seven.

Eight-year-old David went into great detail telling his parents about his swimming accomplishment—he dove off a high dive, swam underwater all the way across the pool, and was the best swimmer in his class. David's parents were quite upset when they checked with the swimming instructor and found out their son had made up this tall tale. They were relieved to know that this exaggeration is quite common for eight-year-olds and that they were not rearing a habitual liar.

Nine-year-old Davina has the ability to state her opinion clearly in conversations with her parents. On Saturday she told them why she thought it was unfair for her mother to make her stay home and help clean the house but let her older brother go to a friend's house for the day.

COGNITIVE DEVELOPMENT

Most eight-year-olds are capable of abstract thinking that involves, for example, seeing how objects are alike and different. They can recognize the views of others. They understand the idea of numbers. They can picture in their minds a series of actions, such as going on an errand and returning. They can visualize events without needing the concrete experience of doing them.

Nine-year-olds' abstract reasoning ability is similar to that of eight-year-olds. They can use logical thinking to apply the rule that the amount of water in one large container stays the same even if you pour it into several small containers.

Eight-year-old Davina is shown two identical balls of clay. The teacher rolls one ball into a long thin shape and asks Davina if there is more clay in the long piece or the round ball. Davina says that the amount of clay is the same in each. This is an example of concrete reasoning that Davina has attained. At age five or six, Davina would have thought one piece was bigger because it was longer or fatter; she didn't have the necessary abstract reasoning ability that she gained by age eight.

MORAL/ETHICAL DEVELOPMENT

Eight-year-olds are usually truthful about things they consider important. Most can differentiate fact from fiction despite their tendencies to boast, brag, and tell tall tales. Typical eight-year-olds want to be good. They are aware of two opposing forces of good and evil. They usually obey adults. They try to do right most of the time and love praise for this.

Eight-year-old David memorized the Ten Commandments in Sunday school. Obeying them was very important to him.

Nine-year-old Davina was quick to tell her parents that she had accidentally broken a glass in the bathroom. She didn't want them to think she did it on purpose.

Eight- and nine-year-olds tend to see moral behavior in terms of rules to be obeyed. They have a "Ten Commandment" way of thinking about rules. Most nine-year-olds think in terms of right and wrong. They want to do right and many are able to apologize when they do wrong. They have great interest in fairness, particularly regarding punishment. Group standards are often more important to them than parental standards. Honesty and truth become part of their vocabulary. They are now developing a sense of ethical standards and want to live up to them. Consciences are developing.

SOCIAL/EMOTIONAL DEVELOPMENT

Erik Erikson refers to the dominant stage of middle and late childhood as industry versus inferiority.[5] Children become interested in how things are made and how they work. When children are encouraged in their efforts to make and build and work, their sense of industry increases. If parents and teachers frequently criticize, put down, or scold children for "creating a mess" in their industry efforts, children may develop a sense of inferiority.

> A primary need of children is the development of a sense of competence. Competence is the child's ability to deal effectively with the world . . . . Children ages 6 to puberty develop competence by being successful at something.

They are industrious and want and need to become work-ers. Children earn recognition by producing things. They want to learn the skills that adults have. This period is a socially-decisive stage since industry involves not only making and doing things but doing things beside and with other people.[6]

Peer friendships are of primary importance at this time. Having best friends and spending time with them takes priority. Boys tend to play in a large group; often this play is competitive with winners and losers. Girls are more likely to play in small groups or pairs, and their play is usually less competitive. They like to sit and talk with friends. They usually take turns in play activity.

Boys are usually more physically aggressive than girls. Girls' aggression is often more secretive and may be expressed by excluding another girl from the friendship group.

Davina likes to have her friends come over and spend the night. Much of their time is spent in conversations about relationships—being liked by other children.

David also likes to have his friends over to spend the night. Their activities include competitive computer games, playing ball with neighbor boys, and riding bikes.

Practical Exercise

Describe two of the children in your class.

1. First child: Name _____ Age _____

• Describe his/her personality.

- In what ways is he/she similar to the characteristics listed above?

- In what ways different?

- What activities does he/she enjoy?

- What are his/her strengths (things he/she can do well)? What are his/her difficulties (things he/she has a hard time doing)?

- What are some ways you can help him/her express strengths?

- How well do you think you understand this child? (check one)

Very well _____ Well _____ Average _____ Not Well _____

- What do you think are his/her main needs at this age?

2. Second child: Name _____ Age _____

• Describe his/her personality.

• In what ways is he/she similar to the characteristics listed above?

• In what ways different?

• What activities does he/she enjoy?

• What are his/her strengths (things he/she can do well)? What are his/her difficulties (things he/she has a hard time doing)?

• What are some ways you can help him/her express strengths?

• How well do you think you understand this child? (check one)

Very well _____ Well _____ Average _____ Not Well _____

• What do you think are his/her main needs at this age?

Teaching Suggestions

1. Refer to the general recommendations for teachers of all ages given in the "General Teaching Suggestions" of chapter 8.

2. Nurture a faith and trust in Jesus. Teach the biblical view of people: (1) We are made in the image of God. (2) We are all sinners who need forgiveness. Teach the good news that Jesus loves us and wants to have a personal relationship with each of us.

3. Practice prayer and Bible study methods that fit the needs of third and fourth graders. Use varied activities that include group activities. Be alert for one-on-one teachable moments, such as when a child asks questions, makes a personal statement, or shows particular interest in an activity or subject.

4. Develop a sense of competence in your children by utilizing their strengths and abilities. Try to discover each child's gifts and strengths. Provide opportunities for children's gifts to be expressed. Point out these gifts to children. This may be the time when a child discovers his or her God-given talents. Be animated and dramatic in your biblical and character storytelling. At the end of the storytelling, pause to let the children make comments, ask questions, and apply the truth to their lives. Avoid over-moralizing after the story. Let the children be influenced by the power of the Bible story. They will usually be responsive to a question like "What does this story teach us?"

5. Try to establish a personal relationship with each child. They all need to know that you are interested in them and that you take the energy and time to find out personal likes and dislikes.

6. Work with the parents and/or caregivers. Ask parents for their input about the child's needs and concerns. Share information with the parents regarding their child's accomplishments in class and what you are doing in class study.

7. Create meaningful group activities. Friendship needs are high. Friendship provides companionship, support, a familiar partner and playmate, attachment, and affection from a peer.

8. Address any bullying that occurs. Bullying can be expressed in verbal aggression such as name-calling, excluding another child, or a group harassing an individual child. There is also a less evident form of bullying in which one child decides to exclude a friend by making statements such as "You're not my friend anymore" and then spreading a rumor about the child so that others will also exclude her or him. Bullying can have a devastating effect on eight- and nine-year-olds, who want and need to be liked and included in a group. The painful effect of bullying can last into adulthood.

9. Focus on helping children practice the spiritual traits of kindliness, cooperation, generosity, and honesty. Emphasize the Golden Rule: "Do unto others as you would have them do unto you." Use role-playing, skits, and storytelling to help children understand and practice these traits at their developmental level. Recognize and compliment children when you see them exhibit these spiritual traits.

Notes

[1] Louise Bates Ames and Carol Chase Haber, *Your Eight-Year-Old: Lively and Outgoing* (New York: Dell, 1989) 1-9.

[2] ————, *Your Nine-Year-Old: Thoughtful and Mysterious* (New York: Dell, 1987) 1-14.

[3] Ibid., 1-14.

[4] David L. Elkind, *A Sympathetic Understanding of the Child Birth to Sixteen*, 2d ed. (Boston: Allyn and Bacon, 1978), 141.

[5] John W. Santrock, *Life-Span Development*, 7th ed. (Boston: McGraw-Hill College, 1999), 34-37.

[6] B. Max Price, *Understanding Today's Children* (Nashville: Convention Press, 1982), 31, 32.

Chapter Seven

Preteens: Ten through Twelve Years (Fifth and Sixth Graders)

Goals for Spiritual Development.

Love God

1. Teach preteens the biblical view of God at the level they can understand.
   - *As Creator*—God made the world and keeps it going.
   - *As Loving Parent*—God loves us, takes care of us, wants what is best for us, and corrects us when we disobey.
   - *As Redeemer.* Jesus is God's Son who loves us, died for us, forgives our sins, and wants us to give our lives to him.
   - *As Holy Spirit.* Jesus lives in our hearts and guides us in how to live.

2. Guide preteens in worship of God through prayer, Bible study, music, art, and drama.

3. Lead preteens to a personal experience and trust in Christ. Share the gospel with them so that they will respond in faith when the Holy Spirit calls them.

4. Help preteens love God by loving God's creation. Help them develop a sense of wonder and awe at the beauty and power of God's world.

Love Others and Self

1. Help preteens love God's church. Teach them the New Testament emphasis on the church as the body of Christ. Help them learn about their local church and their role as an important part of the church.

2. At the preteens' level of comprehension, emphasize Jesus' teaching of the Golden Rule: "Treat others as you want them to treat you."

3. Seek to form an attachment to your preteens. When preteens know they are cared for, they are likely to respond in love to adults and peers.

4. Help preteens love and respect themselves. Provide teachers who love and understand preteens and are able to relate to them. Help your young people sense that they are valued and cared for by teachers, parents, and caregivers. Discover and develop each preteen's particular gifts so that he or she has a sense of industry and accomplishment.

5. Teach the spiritual values of generosity, cooperation, kindliness, and honesty.

    Generosity. Provide preteens experiences in giving. They can be led into acting friendly toward people who are different from them. They can learn to be tolerant, a vital part of generosity. Preteens can be encouraged to think generously outside their own circles. Lead them to give some of their money to the church and other charities, give away toys and clothes they have outgrown, and to volunteer to help others. Our goal is to help preteens experience the joy of generosity versus the selfishness of greed.

    Cooperation. Give preteens opportunities to be helpful. Provide joint activities that foster cooperation. Model cooperation and give them practice in doing things together. Adults can use their speech and actions to show that cooperation is expected. Give approval and compliments when you see preteens cooperating in a task or activity.

Kindliness. This spiritual value emphasizes being polite, loving, and caring toward others. It rejects society's emphasis on children being completely self-sufficient without concern for the needs of others. Excessive selfishness and greed are significant values in today's culture. A focus on the spiritual values of kindness and generosity is a major need in children's religious education.

Honesty. Adults can model honesty in their relationship with preteens. Compliment preteens when they show courage in telling the truth. Share stories that demonstrate honesty and lead discussions regarding the importance of telling the truth.

Practical Exercise

Write at least two goals for your preteens this year.
1. Goal One:

Objective: How we/I want to accomplish this goal.

2. Goal Two:

Objective: How we/I want to accomplish this goal.

Common Characteristics of Preteens

Child behavior develops in a particular pattern. Children go through predictable stages of development. The following characteristics are to help you know what to expect in your children at certain ages. However, each child progresses at his or her own rate depending on personality, health, and how the world treats him or her. An individual child may be at a younger or older level of development.

The following are common characteristics of preteens at ten, eleven, and twelve years of age. The alternating ages of harmony/good adjustment and disharmony/difficult adjustment continue at these ages and into adolescence.

For most children, ten is an age of positive personal and social adjustment. It is usually an age marked by calmness, pleasure, and peacefulness. Ten tends to be the high point of childhood. Ten-year-olds are at peace with themselves and their world. Eleven-year-olds are often quite the opposite. They enter a time of discord and discomfort. They test the limits of what authority will and will not permit. The typical twelve-year-old is more positive, more enthusiastic about life, and more tolerant than the often irritable eleven-year-old.

To understand preteens fully, we need to know about three things—the child's basic personality, what to expect of this child at her or his particular age level, and the kind of environment in which the child lives. Also, we need to discover the moral and spiritual values of the preteen and his or her family.

Ten-year-olds

Louis Bates Ames stated,

> There's nobody nicer than a ten-year-old . . . . [T]he child of
> this age loves his family . . . loves life and shares it enthusias-
> tically with those near and dear. The outstanding thing about
> the typical ten-year-old is a certain goodness, a smoothness, a
> friendliness, an acceptance of things as they are.[1]

Most ten-year-olds love their whole family, enjoy their grandparents, get along well with friends of the same sex, have best friends, have messy rooms, and like school. Play is a major part of their lives. They enjoy doing many things. Fairness is very important at this age. Again, Ames summarized,

> The typical ten-year-old is at heart a very positive person—friendly,
> secure, outgoing, trusting of others and, for the most part within
> reason, trustworthy. Boy or girl still needs a good deal of supervision
> and direction and is usually ready and willing to accept both.[2]

Eleven-year-olds

Typical eleven-year-olds are a major change from the friendly ten. Contrary and oppositional behavior is common. These children often behave like a beginning adolescent. They are energetic and self-centered. They are constantly on the go—eating, talking, moving about. It is difficult for them to sit quietly.

Their quarreling with siblings, rebelliousness against parents, and lack of cooperation in helping with chores or assigned tasks are manifestations of early preadolescent self-assertiveness and self-absorption.

Most parents and teachers want their children to grow up and become strong, independent, and self-sufficient, but their patience can be sorely tested by the resistant, critical, and rebellious behavior of their preteen eleven-year-old son or daughter.

The eleven-year-old is full of contradictions, very "good" at times, then very "bad." They are usually worse at home with their parents. They are often reported to be "wonderful" away from home and enjoyed by adults other than their parents. In away-from-home situations they can be delightful, alert, imaginative, outgoing, energetic, and ready for adventure.

Twelve-year-olds

Louise Bates Ames wrote, "Calm Twelve follows picky, objecting Eleven as sunshine follows storm. Girl or boy is, in many ways, a dream come true . . . . [T]he typical mother will describe her preteen as tolerant, sympathetic and friendly."[3]

Life for the eleven-year-old seems like struggling up a steep hill, while the twelve-year-old seems to be at the top of the hill with the struggle over, enjoying the good view. Most twelve-year-olds are comfortable with their own personalities. It is a nice age to be, a satisfactory time not only for the growing girl or boy but also for adults and other children around them.

PHYSICAL DEVELOPMENT

Puberty is a period of rapid skeletal and sexual maturing that occurs mainly in early adolescence. It includes a growth spurt. Hormonal and bodily changes occur, on the average, about two years earlier in girls (at age 10 $^1/_2$) than in boys (at age 12 $^1/_2$). A girl's first menstrual period now occurs at about age twelve and a half compared to age fourteen in 1900. The first period may occur as early as age ten or as late as age fifteen and a half and still be considered normal. At age ten, girls are about even with boys in size and sexual maturity. Most girls show unmistakable signs of approaching adolescence during their tenth and eleventh years. Boys are of comparable height as girls, but the rate of boys' growth is slower. Because girls are more rapid in physical, sexual, and social development, girls are more sexually aware than boys but usually less outspoken about it.

At age eleven, girls show wide extremes in their physical and sexual development. Some eleven-year-old girls show no sign of sexual development, while a majority of girls have started their phase of faster height growth. The average girl has achieved about 80 percent of her adult stature and close to 50 percent of what she will weigh. By twelve, most girls have experienced breast development.

At age eleven, boys show few signs of sexual maturing. About one-fourth have started their growth spurt. The average boy has achieved a little more than 80 percent of his adult height and less than half the weight he will have at age twenty-one. Twelve is the usual time of most rapid growth in both height and weight. Boys also become more interested in sex during these years.

There is a wider range of differences in the rate of physical growth among twelve-year-olds than among ten- or eleven-year-olds.

Many preteens do not get enough exercise. Childhood obesity is a major health problem for approximately 30 percent of elementary-age children.

MOTOR DEVELOPMENT

Most fifth and sixth graders enjoy physical activities such as running, climbing, skipping rope, swimming, bike riding, skating, and/or organized team sports such as baseball, basketball, soccer, and football. By ages ten to twelve, children begin to show manipulative skills similar to the abilities of adults and can master complex motor skills needed to produce quality crafts or play a difficult piece on a musical instrument. Girls usually outperform boys in fine motor skills and boys tend to outperform girls in gross motor skills.

Eliot and Ella

At ages ten and eleven, Eliot dramatically improves his baseball skills. He likes to draw detailed cartoon characters.

Ella has become an accomplished swimmer at age eleven. She has made strong progress in her piano playing. Last Sunday she played "When I Survey the Wondrous Cross" for children's church.

COGNITIVE DEVELOPMENT

Preteens' cognitive ability includes more abstract reasoning than that of seven- to nine-year-olds. According to the Swiss psychologist Jean Piaget, children move into formal operation thought between the ages of eleven and fifteen. They change from trial-and-error thinking to problem solving that requires deductive reasoning. They can use symbols for symbols in areas such as grammar, algebra, and metaphors. For example, in grammar they can understand that the word *house* is a noun. They use the symbol "noun" to label the word "house," which is a symbol for a building (a concrete object). In algebra, the letters "x" and "y" are used for numbers, which are symbols. In using metaphors, preteens recognize the symbol in a sentence like "The moon is a round chunk of Swiss cheese." Most older children understand that this is only a descriptive way to portray the color and shape of the moon, while younger children might think of it in more literal terms.

Eleven-year-old Eliot was able to understand that Jesus' parable of the Good Samaritan is more than a story about one good person who helped a hurt person; it presents a truth of how we are to treat people in need.

Ella was self-conscious at Sunday school today about how her hair looked. She constructed an imaginary audience. She believed that everyone in the class noticed her appearance and thought her hair looked as bad as she thought it did. In fact, none of the other children or teachers noticed any problems with her hair today.

In formal operations, children can think about thinking. For example, a preteen may wonder what her friend thinks about her. Preteens begin to mature in their thinking abilities and become ready for the abstract thought needed in curriculum areas such as algebra, grammar, and metaphors.

MORAL/ETHICAL DEVELOPMENT

Being a "good boy" or "good girl" is important to ten-year-olds. They usually listen to their parents, teachers, and other adults and try to do "what's right." Conscience development is significant. Louise Bates Ames quotes a ten-year-old boy: "Conscience usually tells me if (something's) wrong, and then I wait till Mommy bawls me out to see if it is wrong." Being fair is very important to ten-year-olds. They feel that cheating is very bad. Eleven-year-olds are less strict regarding morals than ten-year-olds. They like to figure things out for themselves and enjoy freedom to make their own decisions. They are usually good to tell the truth about "big" things. They often know what is right or wrong but may have trouble doing what is right They are subject to "defensive lying"—lying to get out of admitting they did or did not do something if they are ashamed or if they want to avoid an adult's questions. By age twelve, most children can arrive at a right or wrong decision through deliberate thought of the merits for or against an action. They are less impulsive in their decisions. Conscience stands guard and can be quite demanding. Twelve-year-olds are better at accepting blame and telling the truth than they were at age eleven. Usually, they try to be fair.

Ten-year-old Eliot listens to his Sunday school teachers and trusts them when they tell him something is right or wrong.

Eleven-year-old Ella told her parents she had stayed after school to help her teacher. In fact, she had gone to another friend's house without permission. She felt guilty, and later that evening she went to her mother crying to admit what she had done.

SOCIAL/EMOTIONAL DEVELOPMENT

Erik Erikson refers to the dominant stage of middle and late childhood as industry versus inferiority. Preteens are interested in how things are made and how they work. When they are encouraged in their efforts to make and build and work, their sense of industry increases. If parents and teachers frequently criticize, put down, or scold preteens for "creating a mess" in their industry efforts, preteens may develop a sense of inferiority.

> A primary need of children is the development of a sense of competence. Competence is the child's ability to deal effectively with the world . . . . Children ages 6 to puberty develop competence by being successful at something. They are industrious and want and need to become workers. Children earn recognition by producing things. They want to learn the skills that adults have. This period is a socially-decisive stage since industry involves not only making and doing things but doing things beside and with other people.[7]

Ten-year-olds are often described by their parents as happy, sincere, relaxed, and very friendly. Usually, they like their families. They have sudden bursts of affection for parents, freely giving hugs and kisses. However, they can switch to sudden bursts of anger and strike out; these times of rage are usually short-lived. Ten-year-olds love to be with friends and enjoy inviting them over or going to their friends' houses to play.

Eleven-year-olds are a different story. There are sudden mood changes, rudeness, and unreasonable behavior similar to what occurred at five and a half to six years of age. Away from home, eleven-year-olds usually express more positive feelings and periods of being "really happy." They can act silly over almost anything. They often seem afraid to be alone. They don't want to talk about their fears.

Most twelve-year-olds have moved toward a good balance in their emotional status. On the whole, children of this age are good-natured, pleasant, and willing to listen to reason, in contrast to their earlier selves. Emotions tend to be expressed in extremes. Twelve-year-olds tend to love wholeheartedly. They will show great enthusiasm for favorite foods, music, parents, friends, and church. They usually demand less of parents than at an earlier age. They move easily and freely among their peers and most have plenty of friends when they want them. Both boys and girls shift interest from one friend to another. There is considerable boy-girl interest and activity.

Both Eliot and Ella flourish when they are doing something well. Eliot is excited about building a clubhouse in the backyard with his friends. His parents realize how important this is to him. They are willing to allow the mess the boys cause with their carpentry work in order to encourage their son's sense of accomplishment.

Ella's industry is being expressed in a joint project with her friends. They are writing and videotaping a play about helping the poor. They plan to show the video to their church group. The title is "Good Samaritans, Where Are You?" At ten, Ella thoroughly enjoyed a family weekend trip out of town. She especially liked getting to swim and play in the motel pool with Mom and Dad. She did have one brief, angry outburst toward her six-year-old brother when he interrupted her while she was reading her book.

Teaching Suggestions

1. Refer to the general recommendations for teachers of all ages given in the "General Teaching Suggestions" of chapter 8.

2. Practice prayer and Bible study methods that fit the needs of preteens. Use varied activities that include group activities. Be alert for one-on-one teachable moments, such as when a preteen asks questions, makes a personal statement, or shows particular interest in an activity or subject.

3. Develop a sense of competence in your preteens by utilizing their strengths and abilities. Try to discover each preteen's gifts and

strengths. Provide opportunities for preteens' gifts to be expressed. Point out these gifts to preteens. This may be the time when a preteen discovers his or her God-given talents. Be animated and dramatic in your biblical and character storytelling. At the end of the storytelling, pause to let the preteens make comments, ask questions, and apply the truth to their lives. Avoid over-moralizing after the story. Let the preteens be influenced by the power of the Bible story. They will usually be responsive to a question like "What does this story teach us?"

4. Use memorization of Scripture, songs, stories, and skits. Ten-year-olds particularly love to memorize.

5. Use available visual material including video cameras, videotapes, and computer-generated videos such as Power Point.

6. Try to establish a personal relationship with each preteen. They all need to know that you are interested in them and that you take the energy and time to find out personal likes and dislikes.

7. Work with the parents and/or caregivers. Ask parents for their input about the preteen's needs and concerns. Share information with the parents regarding their preteen's accomplishments in class and what you are doing in class study.

8. Create meaningful group activities. Friendship needs are high. Friendship provides companionship, support, a familiar partner and playmate, attachment, and affection from a peer.

9. Address any bullying that occurs. Bullying can be expressed in verbal aggression such as name-calling, excluding another child, gossiping, or a group harassing an individual child. There is also a less evident form of bullying in which one child decides to exclude a friend by making statements such as "You're not my friend anymore" and then spreading a rumor about the child so that others will also exclude her or him. Bullying can have a devastating effect

on preteens, who want and need to be liked and included in a group. The painful effect of bullying can last into adolescence and adulthood.

10. Focus on helping preteens practice the spiritual traits of kindliness, cooperation, generosity, and honesty. Emphasize the Golden Rule: "Do unto others as you would have them do unto you." Use role-playing, skits, and storytelling to help preteens understand and practice these traits at their developmental level. Recognize and compliment preteens when you see them exhibit these spiritual traits.

11. Help relate church behavior to behavior in daily life. Preteens' moods and behavior change depending on their environment at any given time. They tend to be inconsistent. Don't expect too much maturity. Work toward relating what they learn at church to other situations using role-playing, discussions, repetition, and assignments.

Notes

[1] Louise Bates Ames, Frances L. Ilg, and Sidney M. Baker, M.D., *Your Ten- to Fourteen-Year-Old* (New York: Dell, 1988), 21-27.

[2] Ibid., 44-53, 59-76.

[3] Ibid., 77-109.

[4] John W. Santrock, *Life-Span Development*, 7th ed. (Boston: McGraw-Hill College, 1999), 34-37.

[5] B. Max Price, *Understanding Today's Children* (Nashville: Convention Press, 1982), 31.

Chapter Eight

Applying Effective Teaching Methods

This chapter provides examples of effective teaching of preschool and elementary-aged children. I interviewed several experienced and skilled children's ministers and teachers and asked them to respond to these two questions: What are effective teaching methods to use with children of different ages? What are some examples of effective teaching using these methods?

I thank my good friend Darlene Koch for her contribution. Darlene has over thirty-five years of experience as a Children's Minister, a state director of children's ministries in Oklahoma, and a nationally-known conference leader and teacher trainer. I know Darlene as a great lover of children and as my longtime friend.

I thank Jennifer Strubhar, Children's Minister at my home church in Oklahoma City. Jennifer is a gifted and caring teacher whom our children, teachers, and parents adore. I see weekly evidence of how the children are growing and developing in their spiritual lives.

I thank Deborah Friant, a skilled elementary school principal, experienced church lay minister, and friend, for sharing her expertise in effective teaching methods and preventing behavior problems.

The prerequisite for effective teaching is a caring teacher. Children sense whether we love and respect them, "warts and all." Methods are the tools that caring teachers use to help children grow "in wisdom and in strength and in favor with God and others" (Luke 2:52b).

General Teaching Suggestions

1. Arrive early. Have your room arranged and be ready to welcome children when they come to your room.

2. Before you start class, take each child's "mood temperature." Take fifteen to thirty seconds to observe whether a child is smiling, excited to be there, shy, bashful, clinging to a parent, crying, mad, or sad. Is the child eager to participate? Does she need time to adjust to the room and then explore/participate? Is he in a cooperative or uncooperative mood?

3. Consult with the parents and/or caregivers as often as possible. Check with them regarding recent events. Examples: "How is Megan today?" "Is there anything I need to know or do for Jonathan today?" Give verbal feedback to parents. Offer them children's take-home leaflets or activity sheets to keep them informed about today's class.

4. Attend and respond to each child. A teacher's valuable gift to a child is time and attention. Attending involves looking at the child and observing the child's behavior. Lean forward to show interest. Responding involves giving verbal comments that summarize your observations, being involved in the child's activity, and/or including the child in your teaching activity. Examples of verbal comment: "Claire, you're doing a good job drawing the picture (reading the Bible verse, helping with the project)." "Noah, you seem unhappy (bored, sad) today. You're sitting by yourself with your head down. Can I help?"

5. Use multi-sensory teaching techniques. Children need to use as many senses as possible in learning. Senses to include:

Visual—Sight: Show children.
Auditory—Sound: Tell children.
Tactile—Touch: Let children touch objects and people.
Kinesthetic-Movement: Include action songs and games, role-playing, and projects.
Olfactory—Smell: Use pleasant odors such as food or flowers.

6. Provide sameness and routine in the classroom. Most children's lives are busy and include frequent changes in activities and caregivers. Stress reactions are common in today's children. By providing the room arranged as it was last week, toys and materials in the same places, and a routine schedule, you offer security, predictability, and comfort to the children. You offer them the same kind of comfort you feel at home in your favorite chair or room. Sameness doesn't mean boring activity. Sameness provides predictability regarding what the child can expect today. Within this sameness you can add all the creativity and adventure needed to help the children learn. Routine is like the walls and floors of a room. Creativity and exciting activities are like the furniture and decorations that make a room inviting.

Birth through Five Years Old

Darlene Koch shared these words of wisdom. Children are listening, observing, and learning from their teachers. They will imitate what you do. If you are calm, they learn this from you. If you are hurried and upset, the children will sense this and become more easily upset. You are the Bible from which the children learn.

Provide trust and security for young children and their caregivers. As Darlene said, "Be preschool friendly." This means having adults to greet children in the hallway, reception area, and classroom. "Have somebody there for parents to see that the church values preschoolers." Darlene strongly recommends having some men in the preschool area in addition to the women workers.

Make the physical setting safe and age-appropriate. Make sure baby beds and furniture meet safety standards. A skilled teacher invites the parents of infants and toddlers to explore the room and see the items used in the care of their children. At the end of class, share with parents and caregivers the activities their children did today. Include information on feedings and diaper changings for younger children. Share something specific that the children enjoyed. Keep parents informed and give them regular feedback.

Teachers need to dress comfortably so they can get on the floor and be at the children's level. Children will move around. They don't have to sit in order to learn. Let the children explore the different areas of the room. Children can work in small groups on different activities. They learn by doing, observing, and repeating.

With preschool children, the best teaching is teaching on the go. Be available to observe a child's play and ready to respond when the child desires interaction. Master teacher Willa Ruth Garlow is quoted as explaining why she got down on the floor with her children: "I'm crawling around on the floor waiting for the teachable moment."

A child looks out the window and sees birds flying and landing on the grass. The child is fascinated by the "birdies." The teacher notices and observes, "Those are beautiful birds. Who made the birds?" The child says, "God did." The teacher responds, "That's right. God made the birds. God made them so beautiful."

At snack time, you can help children say and sing "thank-you" prayers. Children's prayers are practical. They tend to name the items they see on the table. Typical prayers are "Thank you, God, for the juice and the crackers. Amen." "Thank you, God, for Mommy, Daddy, my sister, my doggie, my bear . . . ."

You can have discussions about nature. If children are eating apple slices, the teacher can ask, "How did this apple grow? Who made the apple? God makes apples to grow."

The child's interest at a given moment can be a teaching opportunity for the teacher who is observing, available, and interruptible when the child seeks adult help or attention.

Preschool through Seven Years Old

Jennifer Strubhar made these recommendations for teachers:

1. *Be well prepared.* Greet the children at the door. As soon as they walk into the room, introduce today's lesson with a craft or activity that relates to the lesson theme. For many families, getting ready for church on Sunday can be harried. It is difficult for the teacher to have the classroom set up and ready for the children as they arrive.

First year teacher Jeannie Jones has a good way to organize her first- and second-grade class. A mother of five active children, Jeannie plans on Wednesday evening. She arranges her classroom and has everything ready for Sunday morning. Jeannie says, "On Sunday morning, I don't want my Sunday school lesson to be the last thing I'm thinking about" as she is involved getting her children dressed and ready for church.

2. *Let kids be creative.* Teachers who feel they are not particularly gifted in some areas, such as music or arts and crafts, may worry that they won't be good teachers. Give suggestions for hands-on craft projects for the children. Expect fun and learning instead of perfection from the artwork. Children don't expect you to be an artist. They will enjoy having you there to watch and help them be creative. Share what you have to give.

3. *Use the teaching materials and plans available in your curriculum material. FaithSteps* curriculum from Smyth & Helwys Publishing has excellent how-to material.

Regarding musical ability, Jennifer remarked, "I have always loved to sing, but I don't have a great voice. I have a great time singing with the kids. They are wonderfully forgiving; the kids have never complained about my voice."

Jennifer recommended an effective method for telling Bible stories to a large group. The key is to involve children's participation and activity. " First, I tell them the Bible story in a very enthusiastic way as if I am hearing it for the first time, using statements and question like 'You're not going to believe this part' or 'What do you think happens next?' Then I get the kids to come up and retell the story by acting it out. They know this is coming and consequently listen very carefully so that they can be chosen to help act it out. Sometimes we let two or three groups have a turn to retell the story."

For children under six, hands-on learning methods are best. Three main methods are songs, stories, and finger play. Jennifer described the use of singing in children's church. "As the children arrive, we begin singing very active songs where the children are out of their seats dancing, marching, and doing actions with songs. We slowly make a transition to more calming songs" that prepare the children for story-telling, a puppet show, or another activity.

Younger children enjoy listening to people read to them. Use age-appropriate books that have good art and illustrations. Be an enthusiastic reader. Children like sound effects in storytelling. They love a good story. Make Bible stories come alive for your children.

Examples of finger play include motions you use in singing, games such as "touch your chin, touch your toes," play with non-hardening clay or play dough, water play, finger puppets, drawing and coloring, and simple finger painting.

Eight through Twelve Years Old

In planning a unit or lesson, remember that you are teaching specific children more than teaching the lesson. Plan for flexibility in your teaching. If children show lack of interest or boredom, be prepared to redirect the study. Have a question-and-answer time. Ask for children's involvement. Look for signs of interest and redirect today's study based on the children's reactions.

Deborah Friant emphasized the value of planning. "The bottom line is to have a plan. It is better to over-plan than under-plan. It is hard to know how long it will take to do an activity." A teacher may plan for an activity to take fifteen minutes and find that most of the children are through in five minutes. Deborah told of a teacher who used flexi-ble planning on a snowy day. The children were uninterested in the activity she had planned. They were restless and excited about seeing the snow falling. Their teacher used plan B. She had the children put their coats on, then took them outside to touch the snow, taste the snow, and make snow angels. When the children came inside, they talked about their experiences, asked questions about how snow was made, and crafted paper snowflakes. They were interested in the teacher's explanations. The children went from restless and disinter-ested to highly interested and involved in learning about weather and nature. Such an experience in Sunday school would offer opportunities to talk about nature, how God works in nature, and how "wondrously made" is God's world.

Plan ahead by having several options in mind that give children a choice of activities. Remember that children learn best when they are involved in an activity based on their developmental level. Sensory stimulation is important: sight, sound, touch, taste, movement, and smell. When children are engaged and interested in what's happening, you are not likely to face many discipline problems.

Darlene Koch described master storyteller Oneta Webb telling the story of Noah. Oneta made the story come alive. She told the story with emotion and engaging dialogue: "Mr. Noah said, 'God told me to build a big boat; it's called an ark.' Mrs. Noah said, 'How are you going to build this boat? And why does God want you to do this?'"

During the story, Oneta used questions to keep the children's interest and inspire their thinking. She stopped at the end of the story. She didn't moralize. She became silent. She waited for the children to respond and to ask questions. After a short silence, the children began to share their thoughts and feelings. Next, she asked the children what part of the story they liked best. She then offered the children an opportunity to role-play the story, draw a picture, or pose a scene related to the story. The children became the characters and lived out the story.

Jennifer Strubhar's method of retelling the story and role-playing could be effective in telling the story of Noah or other Bible characters. The teacher tells the story while the children listen intently. At the end the children have the opportunity to retell the story by acting it out.

Jennifer gave an example of applying a lesson outside the Sunday school class. She and her husband Rustin taught a lesson on "Who is my neighbor?" They led the children to think of people whom we are responsible to help, aside from family and church members. This led to community mission projects including boxing food for a hungry children's charity and a visit to a retirement home where they sang songs and did a craft project with the elderly residents. The teachers don't have to do all the work in such mission projects. They can recruit help. They can ask parents or other church members to help carry out the projects.

Jennifer shared this example of a Sunday school lesson about Elijah and Elisha from 2 Kings 2. Elijah and Elisha have become close friends, and Elisha is to take over Elijah's job after Elijah is taken up to heaven on a chariot of fire. Elisha is jeered by town youth, and Elisha calls down a curse on them in which two bears come out of the woods and maul the youth. This lesson is one of the children's favorites. Three months after the lesson the children still ask and talk about the story of the bears in 2 Kings.

The Bible story was presented using two puppets: Faith, the puppet who has all the answers, and Christian, the puppet who asks questions the children may have but aren't sure it's okay to ask. During the storytelling, the children became attached to the good friends Elijah and Elisha. They were sad when Elijah was taken up and Elisha was alone. The children became upset about how Elisha was treated by the kids who called him names. They liked the ending in which the bears came and mauled the mean kids. The puppets made the story so interesting that the children became involved in the story, particularly the part about the bears. The children then acted out the story in animated ways.

Their teachers led in a discussion of the story, asking questions like the following. "What can we learn from this story?" "Did you get mad at the kids for teasing Elisha? Is it bad for us to make fun and tease people?" "Were you glad that the bears killed the mean kids?" "If you do something bad like these kids, are you afraid God will hurt you like he did with the bears?" "Will God help you if someone says bad things to you?" "Will God help you when you are scared?" This little known Bible story brought out strong feelings in the children—love, attachment, sadness, fear, and revenge. It led to meaningful discussion between teachers and children. It was so meaningful that the children still ask if they can hear the story about the bears again.

Darlene Koch provided this example of a student-involved unit of study for preteens:

SUBJECT: LEARNING ABOUT OUR CHURCH

The teacher lays the groundwork for a series in which the preteens discover how their church came to be. The teacher refers to the New

Testament Scripture passages in which Jesus created the church so that we can learn about him and tell others about him.

The teacher suggests that the children do a four- to six-week research project about their church. They can present their findings in a video or booklet form. In the first session, teachers begin the discussion with research questions and have children come up with their own questions. Children are assigned questions to research individually or in small groups.

Typical questions to research:

- *Church History.* How old is our church? How did our church get started? How many people started the church? How many members does the church have today?
- *Staff.* Who was our first pastor? Is he/she still living? If so, where? How do we choose a pastor? Who is our pastor now? What does he/she do? Who are our other staff members? What do they do?
- *Worship.* How do we decide how to worship in music, prayers, Bible reading, special music, and sermon?
- *Ordinances.* How do we do baptism and communion?
- *Church membership.* How do you become a member of our church? What does it mean to be a member of our church? What is my responsibility to the church? How is our church alike and different from other churches? Why aren't we all the same? Why do we have differences?

Ask open-ended questions that arise during the discussion and assignments. The teachers provide guidance to the children as how to find answers to their questions—interviews, church library, etc.

On subsequent Sundays, have children work in small groups on their projects and discuss their findings, with teachers serving as resources. Have children decide on their presentation format such as using a video camera presentation, a computer presentation with PowerPoint, or an illustrated booklet with photos, articles, and art.

Have the children do their presentation in Sunday school. If possible, have a presentation for a larger group—the Sunday school department or church-wide group.

This example utilizes several methods of multi-media presentations: writing, art, video production, and interviewing. It is based on older children's curiosity, ability to research and investigate, and self-directed learning inspired by the children's motivations and questions. Children learn best from doing an activity rather than listening passively. They are encouraged by working together as a team for a common good.

Practical Exercise

1. List two methods you have used effectively in teaching your children.

2. Write a brief description of an effective teaching plan you have used and/or plan to use.

Chapter Nine

Discipline

Discipline is not a punishing word. Discipline refers more to teaching and learning than to stopping undesired behavior. It comes from the same Latin word as "disciple." To be a disciple is to be a learner or student. To discipline a child is to help him or her learn important rules about life. As the writer in Proverbs states, "teach your children right from wrong, and when they are grown they will still do the right" (Prov 22:6). We are to teach moral and spiritual values. Discipline involves teaching right and wrong behavior.

In this chapter, I will focus on the behavioral aspects of discipline. The emphasis will be on preventing and managing behavior problems.

Preventing Behavior Problems

Prevention is the preferred strategy. It involves actions that teachers and parents/caregivers can practice to foster children's growth and coping ability. It is creating a classroom atmosphere of love and limits. It is providing a setting that says, "This is your room. Come be a part of us." The activities are based on the developmental needs of the children. Teachers convey, "We're so glad to see you. Welcome. We're here for you."

The rules are few, clear, and consistently applied. I recommend as few rules as possible but as many as are necessary. Have rules that emphasize "dos," not just "don'ts." If children know and have practice in what we want them to do, teachers will spend less time telling them "don't" or "stop."

SIX RECOMMENDED PREVENTION STRATEGIES

1. *Knowledge.* Become informed of your children's stages of development. Your concerns and worries can decrease when you know whether a child's behavior is within "the normal range" for his or her age and abilities. You will also be better able to recognize serious behaviors that need early intervention.

2. *Understanding.* Observe and listen to your children. Take their "emotional temperatures" as to their moods, energy level, successes and failures, and joys. Sometimes children are eager to tell you about their day. Sometimes they answer the question "How is your day?" with one-word responses such as "okay" or "fine." When they don't want to talk, observe their body language and actions.

    Learn a child's temperament, strengths, and weaknesses. Communicate understanding to the child. For example, "You took really excited and happy today." "I can tell that you are unhappy about something today. You have a frown on your face and you yelled when I asked you to help me." Give your children the precious gift of accurate understanding.

3. *Acceptance.* Communicate acceptance of your children even when they are more difficult. Give children a sense of security by showing your unconditional love, even when they are unpleasant or in a negative mood. Understanding and acceptance provide a setting in which children are more likely to respond positively to your discipline.

4. *Respond.* Act based upon what you determine to be the children's needs at any given time. Children are good at communicating what they need from us. Trust your ability to read what the child needs today—more limits, more freedom, more affection, more time with you, more time alone, or more responsibility.

5. *Consistency.* Be predictable. When children say, "My teacher does it this way," it means they can count on you to be predictable. Our children need the stability of consistent treatment by their caregivers. Children learn to adjust to strict teachers, democratic

teachers, and lenient teachers, but they have difficulty when the rules are inconsistently applied.

6. *Resources.* Use all the teacher resources available to help you help your children. Consult with other teachers, parents, and staff members so you don't feel like you are supposed to have all the answers. Don't hesitate to talk with your children's minister and/or department director. I hope this book will be a good resource for you.

GROUP STRATEGIES TO USE FOR PREVENTING BEHAVIOR PROBLEMS

I interviewed childhood educator Deborah Friant regarding what teachers can do to prevent behavior problems. She said that teachers benefit most from having children engaged and interested in the session. If the children are engaged, you are not likely to have many discipline problems. Deborah emphasized *planning*. It is better to over-plan than under-plan because it is hard to know how long it will take to teach the material.

Deborah recommended having a routine and being flexible. This may sound contradictory at first. Children need the security of having something repeated each week. She recommended a routine of singing the same song every week. Routine helps create a setting for learning. When you begin a learning activity and you find that your methods are not working, be flexible enough to move to another activity. Go to Plan B or Plan C in order to engage the children in an activity.

Deborah shared some techniques to prevent behavior problems. Transition techniques are designed to move the children from focusing on external events that distract the children to focusing on the present group. It is okay to have noisy activity to help the children transition to the present group focus.

The following are transition activities to help children move to the desired focus:

1. *Get your wiggles out.* The teacher leads group actions. For example, "Let's help Noah gather up the animals and put them in the ark. Reach up and get bird and put it in the ark. Find a bear and put it

in the ark." Continue naming other animals. Let children name one animal at a time.

2. *Use music to get children's attention.* "When the music stops/starts it is time to (whatever you want the children to do)."

3. *Use a rhyming activity to focus attention.* For example, ask children to sit on the floor with their legs crossed, then say the following rhyme.
> Criss cross, applesauce.
> Give your hands a snap.
> Give your hands a clap.
> Put them in your lap.

Use rhythm clapping to create group togetherness.

4. *Get children's attention by making specific requests.* Examples:
> "I only want quiet people to line up. Only quiet people can line up. Wait until every child is participating to proceed. If a child is reluctant, it usually helps if the teacher stands close to the child.
> "If you hear my voice, clap once."
> "If you hear my voice, clap twice."
> "If you hear my voice, touch your nose (chin, ears, knees, toes)."

5. *Try group energizers,* such as these devised by Jeanne Gibbs.[1]
> *(a) Zap*
> Stand in a circle. The leader asks the children to "create some energy" by rubbing their hands together quickly back and forth. Next, the leader asks them to take a deep breath in, hold for two to three seconds, and breathe out. Do two more deep breaths while continuously rubbing hands. Finally, while everyone rubs hands together, the leader says that on the count of three, everyone will make a sweeping point with their right arm to the center of the circle and yell "zap!" This energizer creates energy, while at the same time allowing for the expenditure of energy. Try zapping any person who wants to be zapped, or zap an undesired behavior such as put-downs.

(b) Do After Me

Sit in a large circle. One person begins by entering the circle and making a gesture, sound, or movement (the more ridiculous the better), and then points at someone else in the circle to succeed her. This person makes the same gesture, sound, or movement as the first person and then adds his own performance. He then chooses the next person, who repeats only the preceding action plus his or her own before choosing someone new. The game is over when everyone has had a chance in the circle.

Adjusting to Developmental Problems

All children experience some adjustment problems at different developmental levels. For most children, the problems are mild and manageable. Difficulties tend to occur in a phase that lasts no longer than a few months. The severity level of developmental problems depends upon the child's coping ability, health, and environment—home, school, church, and community.

EXAMPLES

Jean was an only child. Her health was good. Her temperament was that of an active child who thrived on adult attention, tended to be assertive with adults and other children, and often took the dominant role.

At age three, one of Jean's developmental problem was interrupting adults when she was not the center of attention. The severity level was mild.

At age six, Jean had a problem with cooperation in a first-grade class. She "bossed" other children, telling them what to do, and took the role of teacher. She became frustrated when classmates didn't accept her "help." The severity level was moderate.

At age eleven, Jean became upset when she was teased by peers and not included in the "in-group." She came home crying several times one month because of how she was treated by girls who said they didn't want to be her friend anymore. Jean had trouble handling the normal fusses and conflicts among school-age children. The severity level was moderate.

Tim had allergies and ear infections as a young child. His parents divorced when he was four. Tim's temperament was that of a shy, reserved child who tended to be cautious in new situations. He knew how to entertain himself. He excelled in academic subjects, particularly in reading and science.

At age five, Tim had trouble adjusting to kindergarten. In the first two weeks, he was reluctant to leave his mother when she took him to school and church. He cried and said he didn't want to stay. He often said his stomach hurt or his head hurt. The main issue was a conflict of dependence versus independence. The severity level was moderate.

At age ten, Tim did well at school, church, and home. He was well liked by his teachers and classmates, who accepted his being shy and quiet. Tim's best friends were younger than he was. He played regularly with a seven-year-old neighbor. Tim was not a behavior problem in Sunday school, but he tended not to participate with the other children. Tim's parents were concerned that he didn't play more with his own age group. His parents and teachers were having trouble accepting Tim's social development being three years below his chronological age.

Severity is considered at a mild degree level because Tim was not concerned or worried. He enjoyed his friendship with Austin, age seven. Tim was content having one close friend; he did not need a lot of friends.

How can teachers, parents, and caregivers help children like Jean and Tim cope with developmental challenges? The teachers consulted with the parents, learned some strategies that were being used at home, and used this information to help the children learn and enjoy Sunday school.

Jean's parent shared these strategies with her teachers regarding her high need for attention, intrusiveness, and domination of other children. For Jean's tendency to demand parents' attention and to dominate peers, her parents responded with selective attention and approval for waiting. They labeled time periods as "Jean time," "Mom and Dad time," and "Wait your turn time." Time periods began with three to five minutes and increased as Jean progressed.

During "Jean time," her parents gave her undivided attention of listening and giving understanding statements. With "Mom and Dad time," Jean received recognition of praise and compliments when she did not interrupt her parents and entertained herself for five to ten minutes. For "Wait your turn time," they played the game at mealtime of each person having five minutes to talk about his or her day or whatever subject each desired. Jean received compliments for waiting her turn. When she interrupted, her parents received one extra minute to talk.

At church, Jean's teachers employed selective attention, using hand gestures of stop or wait without giving eye contact when Jean interrupted. When she complied, they gave her eye contact and praise for waiting and let her have her turn in talking. Jean's teacher told her she needed her help with certain jobs including arranging the chairs and putting away supplies. Jean received recognition for this non-interrupting help.

For peer difficulties, Jean's parents encouraged her to have one friend at a time for visits to play. This gave Jean, an only child, practice sibling-like time of give and take with another child.

Jean's parents and teachers listened to her complaints when she shared her hurt and frustration at being teased and rejected by peers. They offered advice and feedback regarding children's fluctuating relationships.

Jean's parents asked for and obtained help from her teachers. The teachers encouraged joint activities in which Jean shared a project with one other child. The duties were divided so that Jean did one part and the other child did a separate part. Recognition was given for cooperation.

For teasing, the teacher used class discussion about bullying, excluding, and being aggressive toward other children. The teachers intervened when they saw two girls gang up on Jean, make cruel statements, and exclude her from their group.

Prevention strategies that were particularly helpful for Tim's parents and teachers included knowledge and acceptance. The parents worked at understanding Tim's personality and understanding their own anxiety connected to his early childhood health problems. It was difficult to accept Tim as he was without trying to change his personality from being reserved and quiet to being outgoing and assertive. This was particularly hard for Tim's father, who wanted him to be highly sociable, popular, and competitive.

Tim's teachers often paired him with another child who was small and shy. They did not demand that he take a lead role in group activities. They recognized Tim's artistic ability and used his drawings in large group time. His teachers talked to him one on one at the beginning of class so that he felt included. They involved Tim at his own comfort level.

Managing Behavior Problems

You may teach some children with significant behavior problems. Typical problems include:

1. *Disruptive behavior*—physical aggression, verbal aggression, destruction of property, angry outbursts.

2. *Oppositional behavior*—refusing to obey rules, strong-willed (stubborn), defiant, argumentative.

3. *Helpless behavior*—avoiding challenges, overly dependent on adults, giving up easily, "I can't" attitude.

4. *Fears/Anxious behavior*—nighttime fears, separation anxiety, phobic fears, generalized worries.

5. *Social behavior problems*—conflicts with other children, trouble making friends, dominating other children, cruel teasing, bullying.

Teachers need help in addressing severe behavior problems. What do you do when serious behavior problems occur in your classroom? The most important step is consulting with parents and/or caregivers. When you observe problem behaviors in class, tell the parents by expressing your concerns. Ask the parents for advice as to their suggestions, techniques that work at home, and information about stress or events that may cause the behavior. Parents are likely to be defensive if they think you blame them. Most parents want to know how their child acts in class. Express your concerns and be specific about what the child did or did not do. Again, ask the parents for direction. Tell the parents when their child improves his or her behavior.

You may have children whose parents do not attend your church. Consult with any caregiver who does attend. Phone or visit a parent/caregiver if you cannot talk with them at church. Consult with your fellow teachers. Find a wise, experienced teacher to give advice. Consult with the children's minister or other church staff. Some children may need to be referred to mental health professionals.

Your success in managing behavior problems is largely determined by your relationship with the child and your skill in applying effective techniques. A child responds best to an adult to whom he or she is attached, an adult who practices love for the child. Techniques based on sound principles applied by a significant adult can make meaningful changes in a child's behavior and attitude.

Teachers' Tool Bag

The following are recommended child management techniques. Choose the ones you need to apply to a particular child with a particular problem behavior.

1. Attention Techniques

A child does many things for adult attention, whether the attention is positive or negative.

- *Positive attention*—praise. Examples: "Thank you for putting the toy in the box." "Good job." "I really like what you made." "Thank you for waiting your turn."
- *Selective attention*—acknowledging a child doing desired behavior; ignoring undesired behavior and immediately noticing more desirable behavior. Example: Ignoring a child who interrupts a conversation, then turning to her when she stops briefly and asking her, "Jayne, did you want to tell me something?"

- *Negative attention*—scolding. Be concise and to the point when a child does something dangerous or completely unacceptable. Examples: "Put that down." "Give it to me now." "I don't like that." "I am disappointed that you did that." Sometimes negative attention increases rather than decreases a behavior. A child who is scolded for jumping off the table may like getting a teacher's or parent's full attention and may repeat such behavior. Try to move from negative attention to selective attention as quickly as possible.
- *Nonverbal attention*—eye contact, hand gestures, body language, and appropriate touch. This is a way to show children you notice them without disrupting the entire class. Examples: Leaning forward and watching a child work on a project; touching a child gently on the shoulder; giving a hug.

2. Change of Setting

- *Distraction*—turning the child's attention from one activity and giving the child a different activity or toy. This is particularly effective with young children. Example: A two-year-old child cries because she wants another child's puzzle. The teacher gives her a different puzzle and says, "This one is for you."
- *Acceptable alternatives*—giving the children an acceptable task that refocuses their attention. Example: The children were excited, noisy, and active. The teacher began singing one of their favorite action songs.

3. Time-out Techniques

Time-out is a brief loss of freedom. A child is required to stay in one area, usually a chair, for a few minutes. Time-outs should be short (2-5 minutes) with opportunity given to cooperate with the rules. Example: Mark hits another child. The teacher, Mrs. Horton, immediately takes him to the corner and tells him, " Mark, you hit Tom. Sit here for five minutes." At the end of five minutes, the teacher lets Mark rejoin the group.

4. Logical Consequences

The child's behavior determines when she can have a desired activity/object/choice. This technique consists of doing the less desirable activity (work) in order to do the more desirable activity (play). This is a technique that I highly recommend for all ages of children.

Examples:

"When you put that toy away, you can choose another one."

"When you finish this job, you can choose what you want to play."

"When you do what I asked you to do, you can have free time."

"When you lower you voice, I will listen to you."

"When you apologize for calling me a bad name and ask me in a pleasant voice, I will take you to your friend's house."

"When you finish your homework, you can use the phone."

This technique works much better than threats like these: "If you don't put that away right now, you can't have any more toys!" "If you say that again, you are grounded for a week!" "If you don't do what I asked you to do, you will be in big trouble!" These threats tend to create extra power struggles between adult and child. They also tend to increase anger from both and to sidetrack the job at hand: the child completing his or her work/responsibility. Threats must usually be increased in frequency and intensity in order to obtain compliance.

Logical consequences place responsibility and choice on the child. When she complies, she earns freedom. The sooner he finishes his work/responsibility, the sooner he gets desired choices. The timing of getting privileges is up to the child.

5. Modeling Techniques

This is a powerful means of learning. Children imitate significant adults and children in their lives, for better or worse. Show a child the way you want her to act, speak, and treat others. Examples: The teachers thanked the children whenever they helped. The children began to say "thank you" when a teacher helped them. A teacher modeled excitement and interest in the Bible story. The children became highly interested in the story.

The teacher modeled ignoring Kevin when he stayed out of the group and complained, and he gave Kevin selective attention when he joined in the group activity. The teacher said, "I'm glad that Kevin is here and helping us. Aren't you, children?" The class followed his example; they stopped noticing Kevin's disruptive behavior and included him when he was cooperative.

6. Correction Techniques

This involves requiring a child to practice the desire behavior. Examples: A child is rude to another child. The teacher requires the child to apologize, giving the child the words to say such as, "I'm sorry I called you a bad name. I shouldn't have done that."

Two children are running through the building. The teacher has the children go back to the beginning point and walk to the classroom. She has them practice this two more times to help them "remember how to walk down the hall." The other children are already in the classroom starting their activities when these two finally get to class.

A child colors on the wall with a marker and is required to clean the wall once and then practice cleaning it a second time.

Whatever rule or technique you use to manage problem behaviors, the three keys are *consistency, consistency, consistency*.

Applying Child Management Techniques

1. Aggression

The children were competitive, wanting to beat the other side in any activity. Name-calling was prevalent: "You've got cooties!" "That picture is ugly!" "You're stupid!" "We beat you, you're losers, you're losers!"

What began as occasional behavior eventually happened at least once each week. It was considered a moderate degree of severity. The teachers met and devised an intervention plan using the techniques of changing the setting, logical consequences, time-outs, and selective attention.

They stopped using Bible games that had winners and losers. They chose learning activities that fostered working together rather than competing. *(changing the setting)*

The children were told, "When you go five minutes without calling each other names, you can choose five minutes of sing time or fun time." *(logical consequences)* On a particularly difficult day, this approach was repeated three times. The teachers were consistent with this rule, and name-calling was minimal the next week.

During storytelling discussion, the children participated with lively discussion without competing for attention for three minutes. The teacher said, "I am proud of how well you all are listening, taking turns, and treating each other kindly." *(selective attention)*

2. Separation Anxiety

Two-year-old Jackson clung to his mother and cried loudly when she brought him into the classroom. He cried continually for fifteen minutes. Jackson became distracted briefly by the toys and let a teacher hold him. He played for five minutes, then began to call pitifully for his mommy.

Six-year-old Madeleine brings her favorite stuffed animal with her every Sunday. Each morning Madeleine tells her mother that she doesn't want to go to class and that she wants to go to her mother's class. She sits close to her favorite teacher and seldom participates in any class activity. Madeleine complains that her tummy hurts or that her head hurts.

Separation anxiety is a common response when young children are in a new setting away from the primary parent, usually the mother. Most children become accustomed to an inviting room with children's toys and friendly teachers within two to four visits, but some children have continuing anxiety responses for weeks. What do you do?

Jackson's teachers consulted with his parents. They were told that Jackson had had a negative experience in day care and had become cautious about new situations. His mother's work hours had changed recently and she worked late two nights a week.

Together, they decided to use positive attention and distraction along with desensitization time. Jackson's mother stayed in the classroom forty minutes the next Sunday. She sat in a chair as an observer and watched the teachers lead the class. Jackson stayed close to his mother at first; gradually he began to play in the kitchen section. At the end of forty minutes, Mom told Jackson, "Good-bye, son. I will be back in this long (hands one foot apart)." She left the room and came back in fifteen minutes at the end of class.

This pattern was repeated the next week, except his mother only stayed twenty minutes and then left. On the third Sunday, Jackson brought a bag with his favorite stuffed animals and his security blanket. The teacher had Jackson show her his bag and they began to play together. Mother said good-bye to Jackson. Jackson cried briefly when she left but only for two minutes. His teacher distracted him with a new toy. During class Jackson asked for his mother. The teacher took a play phone and pretended that the mother was on the line: "Jackson, it's Mommy. She wants to talk to you." Jackson took the phone and had a brief pretend phone conversation. He repeated this telephone game several times. After that Jackson's separation anxiety was manageable, except on a Sunday when his mother was sick and a family friend brought Jackson to the classroom.

For six-year-old Madeleine, a teacher-parent conversation revealed that Madeleine's family had moved recently and she had changed schools at the end of the first semester. Madeleine had become attached to her first-grade teacher, Mrs. Horton. She was having a hard time adjusting to a new teacher and to making friends in the new community.

The teacher and parents came up with a workable plan for Madeleine. The next Sunday, Madeleine was encouraged to draw a picture for Mrs. Horton, and the teacher helped Madeleine print a letter for Mrs. Horton. Madeleine's mother mailed the letter the next day. The teachers encouraged Madeleine to sit close to her favorite Sunday school teacher and to be in her small group. She was encouraged to bring pictures and favorite toys to church to show her teachers and classmates. Madeleine's mother stayed in class for a ten-minute sharing. The goal was to bring some comforting items from home to make her more comfortable at church. After a show-and-tell time, these items were placed on a shelf. Madeleine's classmates showed more interest in her and the teacher complimented the children for making friends with her. Her somatic "I feel sick" complaints stopped after three weeks.

3. Defiant Behavior, Arguing

Karen and Jeremy are two strong-willed, oppositional children who make their teachers' jobs difficult. Karen likes to argue with her teachers about assigned activities. She wants to sing when the class is involved in a different activity. She says the activity is boring and begins a separate activity.

Jeremy overreacts to any adult command or instruction. He has a high need to control situations. Jeremy will look a teacher in the eye and say "no" when asked to do something, or he will start an activity and refuse to stop during group time.

The teachers consulted with their children's minister. They asked for input from Karen's and Jeremy's parents, who reported that this same kind of oppositional behavior was common at home and at school. Karen is more cooperative at home when she is informed ahead of time about the day's schedule and what her duties and choices are. Jeremy reacts the strongest at home when his father gives orders in a loud voice. Punishment is usually not effective with Jeremy.

The teaching team decided to emphasize a logical consequences technique along with limited choices for both children.

For Karen, singing was a primary interest. She liked to choose her favorite songs and be the song leader. The next week at the beginning of class the teacher said, "Karen, when you do this project for the whole ten minutes, you can be first to pick out your favorite song and to help me lead it at sing time." Karen seemed pleased with this choice. She participated for five minutes, said she didn't like the activity, and left the area. At music time, Karen picked out her favorite song and told her teacher, "Sing this one first. I'll show you how to do the motions." Karen's teacher calmly stated, "I'm sorry, but you didn't finish the project I asked you to do. You don't get to choose a song today. I hope you finish your work next time." Karen objected strongly and began to argue, saying, "That's not fair." The teacher did not argue back or give Karen any eye contact. She simply stated,

"Karen, that was your choice today," and began the sing time with the other children.

The next week Karen was given the same choice. This time she complied with only one short "I'm bored" statement and did lead her favorite song. The teachers continued to use the limited choices approach, informing Karen of her choices each day: "When you (cooperate, work, do the assigned task), you can (choose an activity, play, lead, do something you like)."

Jeremy's teachers discovered that he was more cooperative when asked to help the teacher or another child and that he needed time to make a transition from one activity to another. Jeremy didn't like to be hugged or bragged on a lot. He did like brief compliments such as "good job," "you're really working on that," or " I liked the way you helped Kelley."

His teachers made a habit of asking Jeremy to do a task or join in an activity. When he refused, the teacher said, "Jeremy, your choices today are, number one . . ., or number two . . . ." When he started an unacceptable activity, the teacher intervened, saying, "I'm not willing for you to do this. That's not one of your choices." With consistent application of this approach, Jeremy improved from an average of five defiant times an hour to one time. To help with the transition problems, the teachers notified Jeremy of what was next and how much time he had left. He was adamant in finishing something he started.

The discipline approach was to tell Jeremy how much time he would have for the project, let him know when there were five minutes left, assist him in putting things away, and making a place for him in the next activity. Transitions were still difficult times, but they improved with this approach.

The child management techniques described and illustrated above are not cure-alls for behavior problems. They are offered as guidance recommendations. Sometimes, there are difficult children in your class. Your calling is to give them what you have—love within limits. As a caring adult, use your best discipline abilities, and consult with parents/caregivers and staff to get the best help for your children.

A double portion of blessings for you!

Practical Exercise

1. List at least two prevention strategies that you use with your children.

2. Will you be able to use some of the transition techniques and energizers described in the prevention section? If yes, list at least two.

3. Identify at least one problem behavior you have experienced with your children. What intervention technique(s) have you used that helped?

4. Develop an intervention plan for a problem behavior.
    • Identify the problem.

    • Severity level: mild, moderate, severe.

    • What background factors may be contributing to the present problem behavior?

• What techniques have helped in the past?

• What resources are available to you in your church? in your community?

• What is your strategy for the present intervention?

Note

[1] Jeanne Gibbs, *Tribes: A New Way of Learning and Being Together*, 4th ed. (Centersource Systems, LLC, 1994).

Chapter Ten

Children with Special Needs

I have emphasized the great need for us to teach spiritual values to all children. Certainly these include those children with special needs. I greatly admire teachers and parents who guide and care for children with special needs.

In this chapter I make general suggestions for teaching such children. I also provide category descriptions of children with physical, learning, emotional and behavior problems and of children who have been victims of trauma.

Remember that special-needs children have the same basic needs of all children. They need attachment to significant adults and peers. They need a sense of trust and security. They need their basic physical and emotional needs to be met. They need a sense of stability and predictability in their lives. They need adults who will provide consistent love and limits. They need adults to show and teach them spiritual values. They need opportunities and guidance in developing their God-given abilities. They need to develop a sense of competence—industry based on being successful at their tasks (work). They need adults to believe in them.

Special-needs children have particular areas in which they need specific help, whether in physical or medical care, educational help, or mental health assistance.

General Recommendations

1. I recommend a team approach in teaching special-needs children. Some of you may feel uncomfortable as their teacher. Others have special skills and callings and are committed to helping these

children. As a children's department, try to identify members of the congregation and community who can train your teachers. Identify those who are willing to be teachers' assistants to provide one-on-one time with a child.

2. Become a student of a child's problem area. Learn what you can about this area and how to treat such children. I recommend this for all age-group classes but especially for classes with special-needs children.

3. Work closely with the parents/caregivers. Ask parents to give teachers help in understanding their child and in providing for the specific needs of their child. Include parents in developing a teaching plan for the child. Check with parents weekly regarding their child's status that week. Give parents frequent feedback.

4. Assess the child's developmental level and limitations. Adapt your teaching to meet the needs of each child. If a six-year-old child's cognitive level is at a three-year-old level, provide activities and toys that are at the three-year level.

5. Find an area where the child can achieve. Every child wants to be successful at something. We want them to be successful in learning, sharing, and caring instead of being successful in disrupting, acting helpless, or feeling hopeless.

Specific Problems and Suggestions

1. Learning Problems
This includes children who have difficulty in one or more academic areas such as reading, writing, math, speech and language, or attention level. Other areas include poor gross motor skills needed for balance, walking, running, dancing, throwing, and catching or poor fine motor skills needed for drawing, writing, and crafts.

Children with learning problems often develop behavior problems, frustration, anger, and a sense of inferiority because they are not able to do well with learning tasks that most of their classmates can accomplish.

Suggestions
Become informed. Know the child's learning strengths and weaknesses. Avoid embarrassing a child by asking him or her to perform a task that he or she doesn't do well. Ask parents/caregivers and the child what things he is good at doing and what he doesn't like. If a child has poor reading ability, don't insist that she read a Scripture passage aloud. Try to let the child express her strength, such as singing.

2. Physical/Medical Problems
This includes chronic illnesses such as asthma, seizure disorders, juvenile diabetes, migraine headaches; life-threatening illnesses such as cancer, brain tumor, heart disease, cystic fibrosis; or medical conditions such as Down's Syndrome, cerebral palsy, hearing impairment, visual impairment.

The stresses of having a child with chronic illness and serious medical problems can be overwhelming to the entire family. Having a church that ministers to their child by welcoming the child and involving him or her in religious education is comforting.

Suggestions
Learn about the child's health problems. Consult with the family to obtain knowledge about the medical condition and special care needed. Adapt your classroom to accommodate the child's physical needs.

Teachers can demonstrate for the other children how to accept the child and include him or her in class activities. If you are uncomfortable around such a child, the other children are likely to stay away and not include the child. The more you are able to see the child as a real person and not as an illness, the more you and your class will become comfortable and attached to the child.

Try to identify one or more members of your class who are caring and sensitive. Ask that boy or girl to be a friend; give him or her specific tasks that include the child.

Develop plans for emergency procedures in case the child has a medical emergency in your classroom. The plan should include teachers, staff members, and parents/caregivers.

In my years of providing mental health care to children with serious medical problems, I have been amazed and awed at the courage, strength, and love of life of such children. Many are able to adapt to their medical treatment and focus on being a child.

I remember a five-year-old girl whom I saw for counseling. Kim had undergone two surgeries in three months for brain tumors. She had some paralysis on the left side of her face as a result of the surgeries. Whenever she was in a public place and she noticed a person staring at her face, Kim would look the person in the eye and say matter-of-factly, "I had brain surgery," and then move on to an area of interest. Children will often teach us how to treat them.

Such special-needs children likely will need extra acceptance, comfort, and assurance by you and class members that they are part of the class.

3. Serious Behavioral and Emotional Problems

As cited in chapter one, at any one time approximately 15 percent of children are in need of treatment for behavior and emotional problems and/or family stress.

We live in a time of anxiety and a time when many children have major stresses in their lives. As a child psychologist, I treat children for anxiety, phobias, depression, bipolar disorder (manic-depression), thought disorder, problems of anger, oppositional behavior, aggression, and situational stressors of divorce, death of a family member, and family conflicts. You are likely to have such children in your church. They need your ministry.

Many of our children today exhibit significant mental health problems. The need is great for professional help for these children and their families. The need is great for our churches to be actively involved with these children and their families, as difficult as this work can be.

As teachers, you are not expected to be professional counselors. Your ministry is to try to understand and guide them with the assistance of the church staff and church family. Ask people in your church who are knowledgeable and skilled in helping children to be your resources. Ask them to provide training and consultation to you as needed.

4. Victims Of Traumatic Experience

These include victims of child abuse and neglect; victims of accidents; victims of natural disasters such as tornadoes, hurricanes, floods, and fires; victims of human violence including shootings, kidnapping, acts of terrorism, and war.

Many children who are victims of such severe stress are diagnosed with Post-traumatic Stress Disorder (PTSD). Symptoms found in such children include:

- Nightmares
- Preoccupation with the frightening event
- Minimal ability to enjoy themselves in play and poor interactions with others
- Difficulty to relax and enjoy themselves
- Hyperarousal and hypervigilance (easily aroused and overly alert)
- Numbing of affect (vacillation between withdrawal, friendliness, and aggressive outbursts; compliant, withdrawn, aggressive)
- Fears
- Avoidance behavior
- Substance abuse
- Acting out sexually
- Occasionally, psychogenic amnesia, flashbacks, and emotional numbing

Suggestions

Refer to mental health professionals and agencies. When you have children who exhibit several of these symptoms or children who tell you of a traumatic event, share that information with the child's family, church staff, and other teachers. If there is suspected abuse, contact the authorities as required by state law. Department of Human Service Child Welfare Unit is the authority in most states. Refer the child and family to community resources for childhood trauma services.

Be a resource to the parents/family to help them find needed services such as mental health care support groups.

In the Classroom

Provide a safe place with the security of sameness in class arrangement and general routine. Offer the sameness of caring teachers who provide a nurturing atmosphere.

Traumatized children respond positively to sameness. They like for things to be predictable and in the same place in your room from Sunday to Sunday. Their world became frightening and unpredictable. They will likely be more comfortable knowing they can count on you to be there and that the classroom will the same "next time." They can become quite upset if you alter their schedule without their knowledge, such as changing rooms, rearranging furniture, and/or altering the program.

Have at least one adult available who does not have a lesson responsibility but who focuses on the children, an adult available for children at any time. Teachers who have one or more special-needs children need teacher assistants who can provide the extra attention and help needed by these children.

Some special-needs children must have a parent or caregiver in the classroom for most or all of a class period. After some adjustment time, the parent usually will not be needed as often or as long.

Practical Exercise

1. Develop a teaching plan for a special needs child.

   • Description of child.

   • Specific needs.

- Child's strengths and weaknesses.

- Teaching goals.

- Classroom arrangements.

- Adult(s) available to help child in class.

- Activities planned for child.

- Resources available for teacher.

- Emergency plan. If a classroom emergency arises, what are you prepared to do?

2. Progress Evaluation

  • How effective has this teaching plan been?

  • What has worked well?

  • What has not worked well?

  • Improvements made in original plan.

The Parable of the Good Samaritan Revisited

As a certain child developed on his journey from infancy to adulthood, he fell among a troubled family, and a fast-paced, uncaring world that stripped him of laughter and joy, beat him with emotional stress, and went off leaving him only half alive and headed for serious problems.

By chance, a certain religious zealot came by and saw the child. He ignored the child's pain, took ten minutes to tell him how to get saved, and hurried off lest he be late for this church meeting.

Likewise, a certain teacher came by and saw the child. She thought about getting involved, but she was busy and, besides, the child was a behavior problem, rude and not very clean. She tried to teach the child, but he wouldn't listen to the lesson and kept disturbing the other children, so she didn't mind too much when he quit coming.

But certain church people saw the child, reached out to him and his family, and bandaged up his wounds, pouring in love and laughter. A teacher helped him grow and flourish in learning love, sharing, and responsibility. The church family provided an inn of happiness. His parents learned how to better care for him.

In the areas where the child still had need, the teacher said, "I'll care for you the best I can, and our church will minister to you with what we have. If you still have other needs, we will seek out support services in the community for you and your family."

Which of these do you think proved to be more compassionate to the child in need? Go and do the same.

faithSteps

Sunday School Curriculum for Preschoolers and Children

> **"** *FaithSteps* places the child at the center of the learning experience. The curriculum treats children with respect, is age-appropriate, provides Bible-based studies, uses educationally-sound teaching methods, and is teacher-friendly. If churches want to provide a quality curiculum for their children, they will choose *FaithSteps*. **"**

—HAZEL MORRIS
CHILDREN'S MINISTER

Call **800-747-3016** today for information and free samples, or visit our website:

www.helwys.com